What's That You Say?

Bright Ideas for Reading, Writing, and Discussing in the English Classroom

Written and Photographed
By Jono David

南雲堂
NAN'UN-DO

What’s That You Say?

Bright Ideas for Reading, Writing, and Discussing in the English Classroom

PUBLISHER: Nan’un-do Co. Ltd., Tokyo, Japan

Download Audio

音声ファイル 無料 DL のご案内

このテキストの音声を無料で視聴（ストリーミング）・ダウンロードできます。自習用音声としてご活用ください。
以下のサイトにアクセスしてテキスト番号で検索してください。

https://nanun-do.com　テキスト番号［ **512155** ］

※ 無線 LAN（WiFi）に接続してのご利用を推奨いたします。

※ 音声ダウンロードは Zip ファイルでの提供になります。
お使いの機器によっては別途ソフトウェア（アプリケーション）の導入が必要となります。

What’s That You Say? 音声ダウンロードページは左記の QR コードからもご利用になれます。

Read by
Anya Floris
Chris Koprowski

for
Mom and Dad,
my first teachers

Introduction

Welcome to *What's That You Say?: Bright Ideas for Reading, Writing, and Discussing in the English Classroom!*

This textbook offers students a unique approach to learning, activating, and enjoying English through the pleasures of engaging with a range of dynamic social, cultural, and historical topics.

Each of the 15 units builds vocabulary, strengthens grammar, stimulates communication, bolsters confidence, and broadens knowledge about many subjects. Fun and varied classroom activities and homework assignments keep students involved with the goals and challenges of each unit.

What's That You Say? is certain to be a meaningful journey and learning experience for both students and teachers alike. Have fun!

LAYOUT AND CONTENT

Each unit is generally comprised of the following parts:

PHOTO TALK is a warm up activity. Students are instructed to look at the photo(s) with their partner(s) and comment freely. Photo Talk is not meant to be challenging; it is meant to introduce the unit topic and to get the dialogue moving. All of the Photo Talk images are directly related to the theme of the unit. Students should be encouraged to focus their comments on the unit topic and to avoid unrelated ideas. However, the most important thing is to get the students talking!

VOCABULARY is a critical foundation of *What's That You Say?* For many students, the most challenging aspect will be vocabulary.

The vocabulary section highlights 10 key words or phrases from the unit reading. It does not, however, cover all key words. Each reading has a number of key words and expressions highlighted in bold. Only 10 of these are covered in the vocabulary section. Students are encouraged to review the other key words on their own. If the students can master the vocabulary section, the other sections of the units will be considerably more approachable. Therefore, there must be an emphasis on vocabulary building.

READ ALL ABOUT IT readings average approximately 420~450 words. Depending upon the class level, the readings may be assigned as pre-reading homework. Doing so will not only save class time, it will more importantly boost confidence because students will perform better in class when discussing the reading. The texts are varied in their styles and difficulty. There is not an ordered progression for the level of difficulty; it merely depends upon the unit.

For lower level students, have them focus on and identify the main points of each paragraph instead of worrying about all the supporting details and explanations. In just 1~3 words, each paragraph's main idea(s) can be identified. Remind students that understanding the main points is generally sufficient to mastering the reading comprehension questions. It is important that they feel a sense of accomplishment at all times.

READING COMPREHENSION is divided into 3 parts, each with 5 tasks: Answer the Questions, Complete the Sentences, True or False. The questions are a mixture of straight informational understanding and critical thinking as some answers must be formulated based upon the context. When sharing answers with the class, allow at least two students to give their answers so that multiple voices and ideas are heard. While some of the answers are "correct" or "incorrect", many are based upon interpretation and/or opinion while others are factual. In the true-false section, false answers should be corrected to make the statements true.

ACTIVITIES generally features three activities featuring a range of tasks and challenges including additional vocabulary building, grammar exercises, informational gap completions, sentence building, opinion sharing, and discussions.

SMARTPHONE SMARTEN UP is a 5-minute smartphone information search about a series of 8 general knowledge or trivia-type questions. Encourage the students to choose questions randomly so as to avoid all the students answering the same few questions at the top of the list.

WHO SAID THAT? FAMOUS QUOTATIONS features 3 quotations by a range of people from around the world. Some of the quotations are simple and literal in their meanings, but others express metaphorical or symbolic meanings. Allow students to interpret them. Also, be sure to say something about the people who said these quotes or allow students to do a quick search.

What's That You Say? is a fact and learning-based textbook but not a source for reference. While every effort has been made to check facts and figures and other information, there may be inaccuracies, some of which may simply be due to our ever-changing world. Any such errors or discrepancies should not impede upon the main aim of this book, however — practicing English. The publisher welcomes corrections which may be amended in future editions.

About the Author/Photographer

Jono David is uniquely qualified to write *What's That You Say?* He has taught English at numerous universities in Osaka and Tokyo, Japan since 1994 including Osaka University and Sophia University. He has a B.A. English Language & Literature from the University of Maryland, College Park, Maryland, USA; an M.A. Modern English Language from University College London (UCL), London, England; and an M.A. Photography from Middlesex University, London, England. He is also TESOL certified and IPA certified (International Phonetic Association, English). As an independent photographer, Jono has exhibited his work in museums and galleries in the United States, South Africa, Israel, Morocco, the United Kingdom, and Ireland. His online photography portfolio may be visited at: www.jonoDavid.com.

~~~ MESSAGE TO STUDENTS ~~~

Dear Student —

Welcome to *What's That You Say?: Bright Ideas for Reading, Writing, and Discussing in the English Classroom!* You are about to embark upon an exciting journey of English learning and discovery.

What's That You Say?: Bright Ideas for Reading, Writing, and Discussing in the English Classroom is not your usual English course book. It includes topics students care about such as social media, travel, taking risks, issues about society, and love. Moreover, the units offer a range of engaging activities so each unit is a unique learning experience. You will also have plenty of opportunity to use your smartphone — because you know you love your smartphone!

What's That You Say? is designed to maximize communicative opportunities throughout every unit and activity. The book aims to encourage communication without judgement of right or wrong answers by allowing students to interpret information in their own way. This approach allows for flexible comments, sharing of thoughts, and expression of opinions.

It is important to speak English as much as possible, even when it's hard. When you speak English, your classmates will too! Using all of your English skills — speaking, reading, writing and listening — to the fullest extent possible is a sure way to improve your English. Remember to ask questions when you are not sure about something! If you can master 70~80% of the readings, for example, you will be doing a great job. Not everyone is at the same level of English, however, so do not worry if you are not sure about something. Your teacher does not expect you to understand 100%. After all, you are not a native English speaker. *What's That You Say?* does require effort, however. The themes and topics are challenging but not out of your reach! You have the English power!

Enjoy English. Enjoy the challenge. Enjoy your classmates!

Good luck!

Jono David

author/photographer, *What's That You Say?*

Contents

Unit 1 The Last Chance for a First Impression

PHOTO TALK Chat freely about the photos with your partner(s). What do they tell you about today's topic?

VOCABULARY Match the words and sentences (careful of word form).

In the spaces, write: the word in Japanese / a synonym in English

A.	split-second	/	F.	trait	/
B.	encounter	/	G.	overcome	/
C.	character	/	H.	perception	/
D.	feature	/	I.	consequence	/
E.	come across as	/	J.	insulting	/

1. Bill and I had an ____________ at a party, but we never saw each other again.
2. I knew it was going to be difficult, but I was able to ____________ the problem.
3. The doctor had no time to think. He had to make a ____________ decision.
4. People are complicated. They have many ____________ to their personality.
5. The car has a lot of new ____________ and is fun to drive.
6. Jill ____________ very cold, but actually she is a nice person.
7. Be careful. Even small mistakes can have big ____________.
8. I know you don't like the boss, but my ____________ of her is positive.
9. It's upsetting and ____________ to hear you speak so unkindly about me like that.
10. Your friend has a lot of ____________. He's funny and really nice.

Read All About It

02

The Last Chance for a First Impression

1. You don't get a second chance to make a first impression, the **saying** goes. Yet, in just a **split-second**, we form opinions of people we **encounter** based on any number of characteristics including age, gender, language, appearance, voice, culture, economic and social status, and the situation in which we meet. Generally speaking, these impressions are quite **accurate**.

2. In the 1700s, Johann Kaspar Lavater, a Swiss physiognomist, believed that a person's **character** could be **determined** from their **facial features** such as the size of the nose and the shape of the eyes and **forehead**. In 1920, American psychologist Edward Thorndike wrote about the *halo effect* which says that one positive quality generally results in a positive impression of a person **overall**. More recent research suggests that shared attitudes and beliefs, such as family or social values, reduce *first impression* bias.

3. First impression bias means to make an immediate decision about a person based on the limited information we have at the moment of the encounter. So, for example, positive first impressions are more likely with a person wearing an **outfit** you like or if the person is **physically attractive** to you. A negative first impression is more likely if, for example, the person **comes across as** insincere or dirty.

4. More specifically, positive first impressions are influenced by personal character **traits** such as acting naturally, smiling, being honest and confident, listening and being talkative, and **presenting oneself** appropriately such as having good manners and wearing tidy, clean clothes.

5. On the contrary, a negative first impression can result from the opposite of these **qualities** and/or also by being too direct, asking very personal questions, talking about **sensitive** topics such as religion, politics, health, or gossip. A negative first impression is difficult to **overcome** because most people are unwilling to change their **perceptions** even with new positive information.

6. Wrong first impressions can have serious negative **consequences**. These may include losing a job opportunity, **exclusion** from social circles, being denied financial services at banks, or having feelings of **worthlessness**. While negative first impressions are difficult to overcome, it is not impossible. Doing so usually requires time and effort, however. On the other hand, positive first impressions can quickly change to negative with bad behavior such as lying or **insulting** language.

Comprehension: The Last Chance for a First Impression

Answer the Questions. Write short answers.

1. How long does it take to form a first impression?
2. What character traits help to make good first impressions?
3. Why don't you get a second chance to make a first impression?
4. What is the halo effect?
5. What are some character traits that can lead to negative first impressions?

Complete the Sentences. Choose the best option or options.

6. First impressions are often / rarely / never right.
7. Johann Lavatar believed character could be judged from jobs / facial features / shoes.
8. Overcoming a negative first impression takes time and effort / money / apologizing.
9. First impressions are based on personality traits / the time of day / the weather.
10. Everyone / Only some people / More women than men make(s) first impressions.

True (T) or False (F). If false, correct the sentence to make it true.

11. T / F: First impressions are always accurate.
12. T / F: Negative first impressions are hard to change.
13. T / F: First impression bias is to form an opinion based on limited information.
14. T / F: People have more positive first impressions of cute and handsome people.
15. T / F: Negative first impressions are not harmful to people.

FIRST IMPRESSIONS VOCABULARY

Adjectives: *Positive* or *Negative*? Write P for positive, N for negative, PN if both.

____ shy ____ bad-tempered ____ cheerful ____ sensible ____ lazy ____ quiet
____ fun ____ calm ____ funny ____ exciting ____ honest ____ intelligent ____ mean
____ moody ____ serious ____ stupid ____ warm-hearted ____ sweet ____ easy-going
____ interesting ____ rich ____ poor ____ sad ____ worried ____ relaxed ____ rude

Add three more adjectives to the list.

FIRST IMPRESSIONS MAKING STATEMENTS

Look at the pictures of the people on the first page of the unit. Use the vocabulary above and the following language to share your first impressions with your partner(s).

A. He/she looks + adjective and + adjective (because + reasons) / but ...
e.g. Alfred looks cheerful and easy-going because he is smiling.
B. He/she seems + adjective and + adjective (because + reasons) / but ...
e.g. Emi seems calm and warm-hearted but she looks a bit shy.
C. He/she appears (to be) + adjective and + adjective (because + reasons) / but ...
e.g. Agnes appears to be quiet and shy because she's turned away from the camera.
D. He/she look like a/an + noun (because + reasons) / but ...
e.g. Katerina looks like a student because her clothes are simple.
E. He/she looks like + adjective + noun (because + -ing reasons) / but ...
e.g. Beverley looks like a serious artist because she is showing her work.

Which of these people do you think you would most / least like to meet? Why?

FIRST IMPRESSIONS JOB INTERVIEWS — SHOULD OR SHOULDN'T DO

Imagine you are going on a job interview. Look at the list below, and decide which of these things you should or should not do in order to make a good first impression. WRITE in the spaces: S = should do, SN = should not do, M = maybe

1. ____ Be on time. 2. ____ Go with a friend. 3. ____ Dress well. 4. ____ Smile.
5. ____ Learn something about the company. 6. ____ Wear sunglasses. 7. ____ Sit up.
8. ____ Relax. 9. ____ Shake hands. 10. ____ Talk quietly. 11. ____ Chew gum.
12. ____ Don't ask questions. 13. ____ Make eye-contact with the interviewer.
14. ____ Ask about salary. 15. ____ Talk about personal problems. 16. ____ Take notes.
17. ____ Lean back in your chair. 18. ____ Wear old clothes. 19. ____ Give clear answers.
20. ____ Lie on your CV. 21. ____ Use polite language. 22. ____ Say thank you.

What other ideas can you add to this list? Write them here:

CULTURE MATTERS. What ideas do you think are different for Japan and, say, America (or another country of your choice)? Discuss them with your partner(s).

SMARTPHONE SMARTEN UP

You have 5 minutes to search for as many of the following answers as possible:

1. Who is a famous Japanese person you have a good/bad impression of? Search one fact about them.
2. What is a product you have a good/bad impression of? Search one fact about it.
3. What is a country you have a good/bad impression of? Search one fact about it.
4. What is a cuisine you have a good/bad impression of? Search one fact about it.
5. What music you do have a good/bad impression of? Search one fact about it.
6. Who is a politician you have a good/bad impression of? Search one fact about them.
7. Who is a famous American you have a good/bad impression of? Search one fact about them.
8. What company do you have a good/bad impression of? Search one fact about it.

Do the facts you searched further support your impressions or change them? Explain to your partner(s).

WHO SAID THAT? FAMOUS QUOTATIONS

Talk about these quotations with your partner(s). What do you think they mean?

"It is only at the first encounter that a face makes its full impression on us."
— Arthur Schopenhauer (philosopher, German, 1788-1860)

"I influence anybody who is able to get through the chaos of my first impression."
— Gary Vaynerchuk (entrepreneur, Belarusian, 1975-)

"Two things remain irretrievable: time and a first impression."
— Cynthia Ozick (novelist, American, 1928-)

Unit 2 Why Learn English?

PHOTO TALK Chat freely about the photo with your partner(s). What does it tell you about today's topic?

VOCABULARY **Match the words and sentences (careful of word form).**

In the spaces, write: the word in Japanese / a synonym in English

A.	throughout	/	F.	primary	/
B.	approximately	/	G.	abundance	/
C.	shrink	/	H.	appreciation	/
D.	inter-connected	/	I.	sympathetic	/
E.	opportunity	/	J.	growing	/

1. John and Mary's lives are so ______________ that they seem like one person.
2. Hana speaks Japanese and French, but her ______________ language for work is English.
3. Traveling is an ______________ to learn and experience all kinds of new things.
4. There are ______________ 14,000,000 people living in Tokyo.
5. You were so kind and helpful to me. Here's a gift for you to show my ______________.
6. The party was great! There was an ______________ of food and plenty of laughs!
7. I was really sad and ______________ when Reika's dog died. I loved that dog too!
8. I put the shirt in the washing machine. It ______________ and now it's too small.
9. ______________ her whole life, Nancy has always enjoyed a rich lifestyle.
10. Wow, your children are ______________ up so fast. They are so big now!

Read All About It

Why Learn English?

03

1. **Throughout** all of human history, it is **estimated** that 30,000~50,000 languages have been spoken. Today, however, there are **approximately** 6,500 living languages, and this number is destined to **shrink** further due to a more and more **inter-connected** world. So why learn a second language? Well, think of a language as a key to opening many doors of **opportunity**. Unlocking these doors can lead to a world of possibilities and experiences. English is a good choice of second language. As the world's most widely-spoken language, even basic English skills can **enhance** your life in unexpected ways.

2. However, English is not the largest native-spoken language. The top 10 native languages are, in order: Mandarin Chinese, Spanish, English, Hindi, Bengali, Portuguese, Russian, Japanese, Punjabi, and Marathi. By speaking these languages, you could **converse** directly to about half of the world's peoples. That's a lot of open doors!

3. There are many reasons to learn English. As the most-widely spoken language, you are likely to be able to communicate with people anywhere in the world. In fact, English is the official language in nearly 60 countries. Surprisingly, even though the United States is the largest English-speaking country in the world, English is not its official language. In fact, the US does not have an official language.

4. English is the **primary** language used for international business, politics, science, technology, and education as well as travel, internet web pages, and social networking. Speaking English enhances job prospects. English also gives you access to an **abundance** of entertainment including music, films, and books. Opening these doors gives you wider cultural understanding and **appreciation**.

5. English is not an easy language to learn, however. It has a challenging grammar, and many spellings do not match their **pronunciation**, for example: though (tho), through (thru), plough (plow), or cough (coff). With more than 1,000,000 words, English is the richest language. However, only about 170,000 of those words are in daily use. Yet, basic English requires knowing only about 1,500 words. Surely, you can master that many!

6. Learning a new language — any language — opens not only doors of opportunity, it opens your mind to understanding different ways of thinking, experiencing, and expressing. Speaking another language builds confidence to communicate with people different from yourself and to be more **sympathetic** to their life experiences while **growing** your own. If you knock on English's door, it will welcome you in.

7. So, that's why you should learn English.

Comprehension: Why Learn English?

Answer the Questions. Write short answers.

1. About how many languages are spoken in the world today?
2. Why are there fewer and fewer languages spoken in the world today?
3. Why is English the world's primary international language?
4. Why is English a hard language to learn?
5. What are some reasons for learning English?

Complete the Sentences. Choose the best option or options.

6. In human history, there have been about 10,000 / 20,000 / 30,000 languages spoken.
7. English is the official language in approximately 20 / 40 / 60 countries.
8. There are about 117,000 / 170,000 / 217,000 English words in daily use.
9. The biggest native-spoken language in the world is English / Hindi / Chinese.
10. The largest English-speaking country is Britain / America / India.

True (T) or False (F). If false, correct the sentence to make it true.

11. T / F: English has more than 1 million words.
12. T / F: Speaking another language gives you a better understanding of other cultures.
13. T / F: The official language of the United States is English.
14. T / F: Learning a second language is like opening a door of opportunity.
15. T / F: English is the second-most widely spoken language in the world.

WHY LEARN ENGLISH THE INTERVIEW

Ask, answer, and discuss the following questions about learning English with your partner(s). Try to give specific reasons or examples.

1. Do you learn English because you really want to or because you have to learn it?
2. What is the best or worst thing about learning English for you?
3. How do you think you will use English in your life?
4. What motivates you to learn English?
5. What is the hardest thing about learning English?
6. Do you think your English now is good enough?
7. What is something you cannot do if you do not speak English?
8. What is something you can do if you speak English?
9. Compared to Japanese (or your native language), is English harder or easier?
10. Do you enjoy speaking English?
11. Ask your own original questions.

WHY LEARN ENGLISH IF ... THEN ...

Consider these "if-then" sentence starter ideas about English. Complete each one with as many ideas as you and your partner(s) can think of in 2 minutes (for each). Write down any ideas.

A. If I could speak English fluently, then ...

B. If the world only spoke English, then ...

C. If my parents spoke English, then ...

D. If I fell in love with someone who only spoke English, then ...

E. If a job I want to do requires English, then ...

F. Make your own original if-then sentence starter about English (or another language).

WHY LEARN ENGLISH SO ...

Discuss the following statements with your partner(s). Share any ideas that come to your mind. You do not have to agree with one another.

1. English is a global language, so ...
2. English can help me get a job, so ...
3. With English, I can study all over the world, so ...
4. English is the world's main media language, so ...
5. English is the internet's main language, so ...
6. English will help me learn other languages, so ...
7. English makes international travel easier, so ...
8. English gives me access to music, films, literature, and more, so ...
9. YOUR IDEA ...

SMARTPHONE SMARTEN UP

You have 5 minutes to search for as many of the following answers as possible:

1. How many new English words are added to the dictionary each year?
2. Which English letter is used least?
3. Which English letter in the dictionary has the most words?
4. What is the most-used adjective in English?
5. What is the most-used noun in English?
6. What English word has three consecutive pairs of letters, e.g. aa, bb, cc?
7. What is the longest word (the most letters) in English?
8. Which English word has the most meanings listed in the dictionary?

WHO SAID THAT? FAMOUS QUOTATIONS

Talk about these quotations with your partner(s). What do you think they mean?

"Language is the road map of a culture."
— Rita Mae Brown (writer, American, 1944-)

"To have another language is to possess a second soul."
— Charlemagne (King of Francia, 742-814)

"A different language is a different vision of life."
— Federico Fellini (film director, Italian, 1920-1993)

Unit 3 Focus on Photography

PHOTO TALK Chat freely about the photo with your partner(s). What does it tell you about today's topic?

VOCABULARY Match the words and sentences (careful of word form).

In the spaces, write: the word in Japanese / a synonym in English

A.	inception	/	F.	fragile	/
B.	keepsake	/	G.	industry standards	/
C.	precious	/	H.	radically	/
D.	portable	/	I.	ubiquitous	/
E.	wealthy	/	J.	impress	/

1. In the 1980s, it was popular to carry around a ________________ radio.
2. Today, smartphones are everywhere. They're ________________.
3. He has worked at the company since its ________________ three years ago.
4. Some things like glass and my heart are ________________ and break easily.
5. To get the job, you need to ________________ the interviewer with your knowledge and skills.
6. ________________ nations of the world should give more money to poor countries.
7. The museum is filled with rare and ________________ jewels and historical items.
8. ________________ are methods, processes and practices followed by members of business, for example, the same rules, sizes, quality, and safety.
9. We ________________ redesigned our kitchen. You wouldn't recognize it!
10. This ________________ reminds me of my childhood. I will never throw it away.

Focus on Photography: A Brief History

1. Since its **inception** some 200 years ago, the camera has gone through various important changes and stages of development. **Consequently**, photographs became increasingly valuable as a visual record of events, personal **keepsakes**, and art. In fact, photographs of family and friends are widely considered our most **precious** belongings. The word photograph is from Greek. It means light (photo) writing (graph).

2. Long before modern cameras, an Iraqi invented the camera obscura, a simple box with a pinhole that **projected** images upside down but did not record the pictures. The earliest known photograph was made in 1826 or 1827 by a Frenchman named Joseph Nicéphore Niépce. He used a **portable** camera obscura to **expose** a special light-sensitive plate.

3. Around this time, other people were developing photography techniques. Louis Daguerre created the daguerreotype by using a unique silvered copper plate. This method became the first **commercially** successful photographic process (1839-1860) in the history of photography, but the process was complicated. At that time, many photo studios opened. Because daguerreotypes were expensive, only **wealthy** people could afford to have their portraits taken. Daguerreotypes were also very **fragile**.

4. In the 1880s, American George Eastman started a company called Kodak. He developed a box camera with a **capacity** of 100 film exposures. The user would take pictures, then send the camera back to the factory for the film to be developed and prints made. This was the first camera inexpensive enough for the average person to afford. It was not until the late 1940s that 35mm film and cameras became cheap enough for the **majority** of consumers to buy.

5. In the 1950s, the Asahi Optical Company and Nikon introduced SLR (single lens reflex) cameras that made taking pictures even easier and with better results. These cameras allowed for **interchangeable** lenses and other accessories. SLRs **proved** so popular that they became **the industry standard** for the next 30 years.

6. Throughout the 1980s and 1990s, the Digital Age swiftly and **radically** changed photography. Because of their popularity and relative low cost, the earliest digital cameras were point-and-shoots. Nikon released the first professional digital SLR (DSLR) in 1988. Over the next decade, Canon, Sony, Fujifilm and other companies did too.

7. We can only imagine how amazed Joseph Nicéphore Niépce would be by today's **ubiquitous** smartphones and other photography technologies. Even the old 35mm film cameras would **impress** him.

Comprehension: The Last Chance for a First Impression

Answer the Questions. Write short answers.

1. What were some of the first major steps in the development of photography?
2. What problems and challenges did early photographers have?
3. What happened that made photography more available to everyone?
4. In the 1940s-50s, what kinds of cameras became most popular for people?
5. How did digital technology revolutionize photography?

Complete the Sentences. Choose the best option or options.

6. In the early 1980s / 1990s / 2000s, digital technology quickly replaced film cameras.
7. The earliest known photograph was taken in 1726 / 1826 / 1926 in France.
8. Early photography was cheap / expensive / reasonably priced for most people.
9. 35mm film cameras became affordable in the 1940s / 1950s / 1960s.
10. A daguerreotype photograph was taken on a silver plate / on film / digitally.

True (T) or False (F). If false, correct the sentence to make it true.

11. T / F: The word "photograph" is French for "light writing".
12. T / F: Early photography was expensive, so only wealthy people could afford portraits.
13. T / F: George Eastman's Kodak company created the first digital camera.
14. T / F: In the early days, taking photographs was a complicated process.
15. T / F: 55mm film cameras were the most popular type of cameras before digital.

Retelling Photography History

Work with your partner(s) to unjumble the conversation below. Partner A, cover Partner B's half of the conversation, and Partner B, cover Partner A's half of the conversation. Write down the order 1~16 in the spaces. When you finish, *speak* the conversation again. Try to add some extra comments. HINT: The conversation starts with Partner A.

PARTNER A

___ Yeah, but they're not so popular anymore. Now people like DSLR cameras.

_3_ Wow. That's a long time ago. I'm sure photography must have been very different back then.

___ I wonder how old photography is. I mean, who took the first photo?

___ That's true. They weren't around until more than 100 years after that guy took the first photo.

_9_ Wasn't he the person who started the Kodak company? When was that?

___ Today, taking photos is so easy. The first photographers wouldn't even know how to use a smartphone camera. Can you imagine that?

___ My parents still have an old Kodak film camera. It's pretty cool. They also have a Polaroid.

___ Well, today, most people rely on their smartphones because they're compact and easy to use.

PARTNER B

___ In the 1880s. His cameras were different. He made small cameras that many people could afford to buy, so photography started to become really popular.

___ That's true. Digital technology revolutionized photography. I wonder what will be the next big thing.

_2_ I think the first photo was taken about 200 years ago by a man in France.

___ It's pretty amazing, huh? I wonder if George Eastman would like digital photography.

___ Wow, I'd like to see that. When Polaroid cameras were released, they were super popular because the film developed like magic in about a minute. Instant cameras are still fun.

___ Yeah, it was. The first cameras were big and heavy. And it took a lot of time to make one photo.

___ I have a couple of SLRs. I used to shoot a lot of slide film. Nikon introduced one of the first SLRs in the 1950s, but I prefer Canon.

_6_ No, I can't. They might not even know how to use 35mm film cameras either.

Genres of Photography

Exercise A

Not every photo fits into a single genre, or type. Many images fit into two or more genres. It depends on the purpose of the photo or how we describe them. Talk with your partner(s) about these genres of photography. What do you think they mean? How many do you know and like or dislike? Try explaining and describing some to each other. For the ones you don't know, ask your teacher — or even another classmate. What other genres do you know?

1. Abstract
2. Advertising
3. Architecture
4. Black and White
5. Cityscape
6. Concert (Live Music)
7. Documentary
8. Event
9. Fashion
10. Food
11. Landscape
12. Lifestyle
13. Long-Exposure
14. Motion / Action
15. Nature
16. Night
17. Panorama
18. Photojournalism
19. Portraiture
20. Street
21. Travel

Exercise B

Look at the 10 most recent photos you took on your smartphone.
Share 3 of them with your partner(s).
What genre(s) do you think they are? Why did you take them?

By looking at the photos on your smartphone,
what genre does it seem you most enjoy? Why? Talk about them.

Exercise C

What genre(s) are these photographs? Talk with your partner(s). Remember, many photographs fit more than one genre. You and your partner(s) may interpret the images differently, so be sure to explain yourself.

1

2

MEMO GENRES HERE:

1.
2.
3.
4.
5.

3

4

5

Reading a Photograph

To truly understand a photograph, it's sometimes important to look carefully at its details. This close inspection is called "reading a photograph". Use the questions below to **Read the Photograph** with your partner(s). Then, read one from your smartphone.

1. What do you see in the photo as whole? Examine the photo carefully.
2. Now, divide the image into 4 parts (top left/right, bottom left/right), and look again.
3. Identify people, gender, age, relationship to each other, what they are wearing, etc.
4. What time of day, year, period, century, or season is it?
5. What are the people doing; what event is taking place?
6. Look at details around the main focus of the photo. What are they?
7. Is the photo urban or rural? Describe these elements.
8. Is there a caption or a title?
9. Is there any identifying information about the photographer?
10. Are there elements outside the boundary of the photo that you think are important?
11. What questions does the photograph make you want to ask?
12. What is the mood of this photograph?
13. How does this photograph make you feel?

SMARTPHONE SMARTEN UP

You have 5 minutes to search for as many of the following answers as possible:

1. When, where, and by whom was the first photograph of a person taken?
2. When was the first digital camera invented?
3. About how many photographs are estimated to be taken each year?
4. When was the first color photograph taken?
5. What does "Kodak" mean?
6. Why didn't people smile in old photographs?
7. Which side of the face is considered better for photographs?
8. Who took the first selfie?

WHO SAID THAT? FAMOUS QUOTATIONS

Talk about these quotations with your partner(s). What do you think they mean?

"When I take a picture, I take 10 percent of what I see."
— Annie Leibovitz (photographer, American, 1949-)

"All photographs are accurate. None of them is the truth."
— Richard Avedon (photographer, American, 1923-2004)

"To collect photographs is to collect the world."
— Susan Sontag (writer/philosopher, American, 1933-2004)

Unit 4 Gender Inequality in Japan

PHOTO TALK Chat freely about the photo with your partner(s). What does it tell you about today's topic?

VOCABULARY Match the words and sentences (careful of word form).

In the spaces, write: the word in Japanese / a synonym in English

A.	disparity	/	F.	burden	/
B.	dignity	/	G.	breadwinner	/
C.	ignorance	/	H.	corporate ladder	/
D.	bear	/	I.	dominate	/
E.	brunt	/	J.	realize	/

1. Lana was embarrassed, but she never lost her ______________ or confidence.
2. Women around the world do the ______________ of the housework. Men should do it too!
3. Mako's mother's illness was a ______________ and caused her much stress.
4. I cannot ______________ to see her treated so badly by her boss. It's so upsetting.
5. In most cultures, men are the primary ______________ in the family.
6. There's an unfair ______________ between the hours women work and their salary.
7. Remi is a strong woman and does not let her husband ______________ her.
8. She's quickly climbing the ______________. She'll soon be the company president.
9. If you are ______________ about a subject, it's better not to share your opinion.
10. She didn't ______________ how much she loved him until he married another woman.

Read All About It

Gender Inequality in Japan

05

1. **Gender inequality** is a legal, cultural, or social **disparity** between the **sexes** that results in different rights, status, and **dignity**. While there are many causes for gender inequality including **stereotypes**, traditions, and even **ignorance**, in virtually all corners of the world, women **bear** the **brunt** and **burden** of these **injustices**. Japan, despite its image as a 21st century nation and technological leader, lags behind many nations in the advancement of women's issues and rights.

2. Japan ranked 120th out of the 156 nations on the World Economic Forum's Global Gender Gap Index (2021), the lowest in the East Asia/Pacific region. The primary reason for this low position is the approximate 25% wage gap. In other words, Japanese women only earn about 75% of what men earn. Worldwide, women make about 77%. There is no truly equal-pay country. The most equal country is Iceland (2021), the least is Yemen.

3. Japan's gender-based roles are rooted in **feudal times** (1185-1868). Women served their fathers, husbands, children, and **in-laws** while men were **breadwinners** and political leaders. After World War II, a Gender Equality Clause (article 24) was introduced in the Constitution which states: *With regard to choice of spouse, property rights, **inheritance**, choice of **domicile**, divorce and other matters **pertaining** to marriage and the family, laws shall be enacted from the standpoint of individual dignity and the essential equality of the sexes.* Yet, women still **lag** behind men in virtually all categories of equality.

4. Though nearly half of all university graduates are female today, most full-time employees are male. More than half of women are "non-regular" employees and are not **afforded** many workers rights such as health insurance, paid holidays, or protection from **firing**. Simply put, women are not given the same professional opportunities as men. They only hold about 7% of positions as a department director; 9% as a section chief; and 15% as a supervisor. If women are denied such positions of leadership, they cannot be expected to have the experience required to move up the **corporate ladder**. Men have a more than **ten-fold** chance of holding these job posts and earning more money.

5. Men **dominate** in professions such as law, engineering, accounting, and medicine while women dominate in more traditionally gender-based roles such as education, health care, and social work — but they rarely hold the highest positions. Men hold virtually all top jobs at women's universities and schools, less than 10% of Japanese companies have women presidents, and only 10% of the Diet's lower house members are female (the world average is about 25%). In all areas, Japanese women are not being heard.

6. It is estimated to take at least until 2065 before women represent 50% of the Diet. Consequently, gender equality in Japan will not be **realized** anytime soon.

Comprehension: Gender Inequality in Japan

Answer the Questions. Write short answers.

1. What is the meaning of gender inequality?
2. What is the main reason for gender inequality in Japan?
3. What is the Gender Equality Clause?
4. What are some professions in Japan that men dominate?
5. What is the impact on women and society if women's voices are not being heard?

Complete the Sentences. Choose the best option or options.

6. Nearly 35% / 50% / 65% of university students in Japan are female.
7. Women hold the top jobs in only about 10% / 25% / 35% of companies.
8. In feudal times, Japanese women served their fathers / husbands / in-laws.
9. Gender equality in Japan is not expected before about 2045 / 2055 / 2065.
10. Japanese men have 10 / 20 / 30 times more chance than women to earn more money.

True (T) or False (F). If false, correct the sentence to make it true.

11. T / F: The gender equality clause was introduced in Japan before World War II.
12. T / F: Around the world, women earn only about 65% of the salary of men.
13. T / F: Women are given the same professional opportunities as men.
14. T / F: Japan ranked lowest in the gender gap in East Asia in 2021.
15. T / F: Women dominate professions such as education and hold most top positions.

GENDER INEQUALITY A STORY OF STEREOTYPING

Read the story once. When you finish, without thinking, make an immediate decision to answer the question. You must answer immediately — your first thought!

> A man and his son were riding in a car when suddenly there was a terrible accident. The man died instantly, but the boy survived. An ambulance took him to the hospital. When he arrived at the hospital, the doctor said, "I cannot operate on this boy. He's my son!"

Who was the doctor? *QUICK — answer immediately!!!*

JOBS, MALE (M) OR FEMALE (F) OR BOTH (B)?

1. teacher ____ 2. nurse ____ 3. yoga instructor ____ 4. taxi driver ____
5. surgeon ____ 6. chef ____ 7. politician ____ 8. hair dresser ____
9. dancer ____ 10. construction worker ____ 11. receptionist ____ 12. secretary ____

GENDER INEQUALITY WORD MATTERS

Gender bias is everywhere in the English language. Look at these words and follow the instructions:

MALE > FEMALE > GENDER NEUTRAL

1. MAN > WOMAN > ______________________
2. ACTOR > ACTRESS > ______________________
3. WAITER > WAITRESS > ______________________
4. SALESMAN > SALESWOMAN > ______________________
5. HUSBAND > WIFE > ______________________
6. your example: ____________ > ____________ > ____________

GENDER INEQUALITY MAKING IT GENDER-NEUTRAL

Read the sentences, and rewrite them to make them gender-neutral.

1. Each student must meet with his professor.
2. The applicant should submit his resume by November 1.
3. All men are created equal.
4. A mailman has to deliver a lot letters during his work day.
5. Everyone can be his own boss, even a woman.
6. A customer should be treated like a king.
7. your example:

SMARTPHONE SMARTEN UP

You have 5 minutes to search for as many of the following answers as possible:

1. What is a suffragette?
2. When did women in Japan win the right to vote?
3. Who was Susan B. Anthony?
4. What percentage of illiterate (cannot read or write) adults in the world are women?
5. Who was Shidzue Katō?
6. What are the average full-time monthly salaries for men and women in Japan?
7. Who is Tomoko Namba?
8. Who is Japan's first female self-made billionaire?

WHO SAID THAT? FAMOUS QUOTATIONS

Talk about these quotations with your partner(s). What do you think they mean?

"A woman needs a man like a fish needs a bicycle."
— Irina Dunn (activist/filmmaker, Australian, 1948-)

"The first problem for all of us, men and women, is not to learn, but to unlearn."
— Gloria Steinem (feminist/journalist, American, 1934-)

"How important it is for us to recognize and celebrate our heroes and she-roes!"
— Maya Angelou (poet/civil rights activist, American, 1928-2014)

Unit 5 Social Media & The Internet

PHOTO TALK Chat freely about the photo with your partner(s). What does it tell you about today's topic?

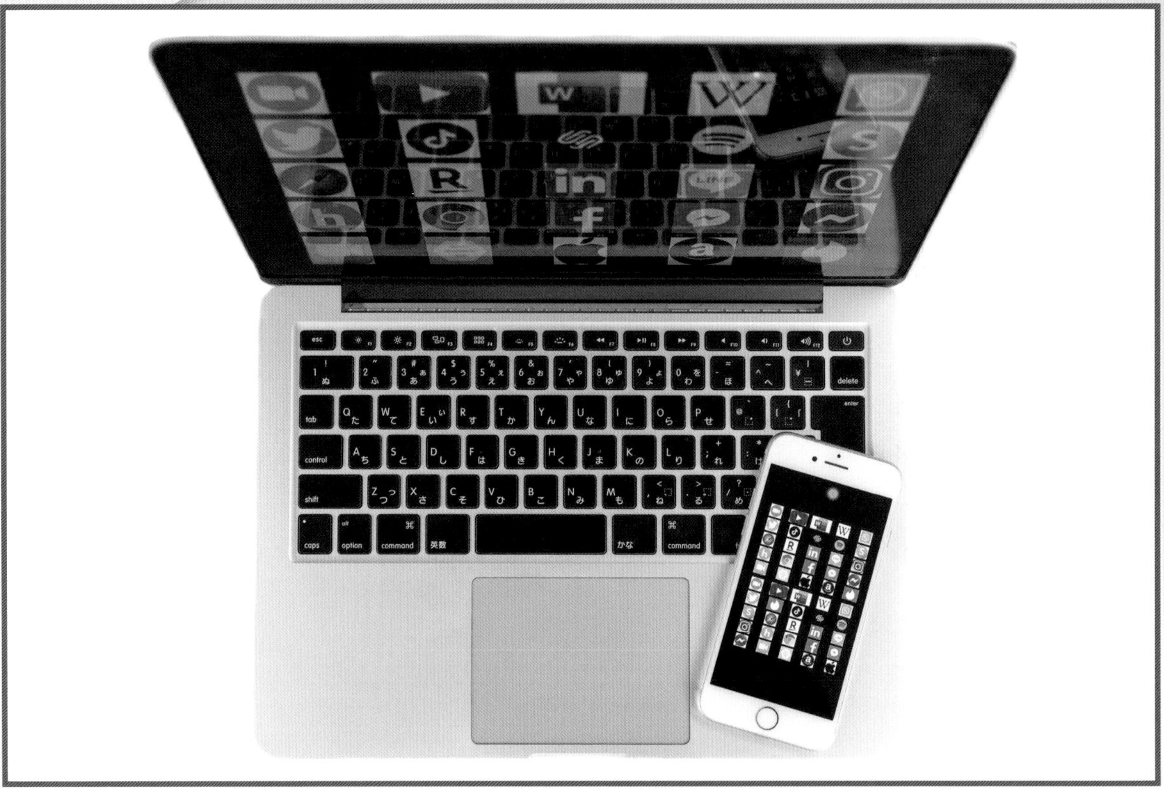

VOCABULARY Match the words and sentences (careful of word form).

In the spaces, write: the word in Japanese / a synonym in English

A.	efficiency	/	F.	apprehend	/
B.	interface	/	G.	prosecute	/
C.	dependency	/	H.	backlash	/
D.	astounding	/	I.	misogynist	/
E.	reliance	/	J.	scam	/

1. People all over the world are connected by ________________ on the internet.
2. Tom and Mary's ________________ on each other is so great. They are always together.
3. Too much ________________ on social media can have negative results.
4. There was a big ________________ to the new law. It was really unpopular.
5. Only a ________________ would be against equality for women.
6. Because of Miyuki's ________________, all of the work was done really quickly.
7. The police finally ________________ the criminal after three days of searching.
8. Social media's ________________ popularity continues to change the world every day.
9. You cannot ________________ someone unless you have enough evidence.
10. If you receive an email saying you won money, don't answer! It's a ________________.

Read All About It

06

Social Media & The Internet

1. The internet became publicly available from about 1993, but it took **decades** of work by computer scientists to develop it. Internet technology continues to **evolve** not only in terms of its structure but also its **efficiency** and its practical uses. Social media is one form of **interfacing** through which websites and applications **enable** users to create and share content or to engage in social networking. Today, it is hard to imagine a world without internet and social media. Like all technologies, however, there are pros and cons.

2. Certainly, one of the most significant pros of the internet and social media is **real-time** communications — live news reports, business conferencing, and personal conversations. This connectivity has made the world a smaller place. Yet, a **dependency** on social media can lead to **anti-social behavior** as people live through their screens.

3. The internet has put more information at our **fingertips** than at anytime in human history. The ease and convenience of "Googling" something is **astounding**. Yet, don't believe everything you read. A **reliance** on **unverified** or grossly **biased** information can have both personal or societal negative impacts.

4. Because virtually everyone has a **digital footprint** today, law enforcement has been able to track, **apprehend**, and **prosecute** more criminals. But websites and social media have also exposed private information to government and corporate **intrusion**. For example, employers often search social media to **gauge** a **prospective** employee. Posting personal views, even bad grammar, can **ruin** one's chances for a job.

5. As internet access grows, people anywhere on the planet can, for the first time, **establish** businesses of all kinds from services to merchandise. Women, for instance, are finding new ways to empower themselves by creating online companies and social movements such as #metoo. Yet, women have faced a **backlash** and online **shaming** by Western **misogynists** and males in traditional cultures. Many hate groups also hide behind social media platforms.

6. Social media can boost one's sense of connectivity, but too much or inappropriate internet time can be addictive and lead to a sense of isolation. Children can benefit from the internet by encouraging creativity, problem solving, and expression, but they are particularly **vulnerable** to online **scams**, cyberbullying, and **sexual predators**.

7. The internet today is **arguably** as vital as water and electricity. Social media may not be as **essential** as the internet, yet no doubt both have **utterly** revolutionized the world.

Comprehension: Social Media & The Internet

Answer the Questions. Write short answers.

1. What is the difference between *social media* and the *internet*?
2. What are some pros and cons of social media and the internet?
3. Who invented the internet?
4. How is the internet helping women around the world?
5. What does it mean to "hide behind social media platforms"?

Complete the Sentences. Choose the best option or options.

6. The internet became publicly available from about 1983 / 1993 / 2003.
7. The internet helps women / the police / misogynists to catch criminals.
8. Real-time communications include live news reports / Youtube videos / Instagram.
9. It took about 10 years / decades / 10 decades to create the internet.
10. Googling information is always / sometimes / never inaccurate and biased.

True (T) or False (F). If false, correct the sentence to make it true.

11. T / F: Too much use of social media cannot lead to anti-social behavior.
12. T / F: A misogynist is a person who supports women.
13. T / F: Today, the internet is probably as important as water and electricity.
14. T / F: Social media can be addictive.
15. T / F: Sexual predators like the internet because they can hide themselves.

SOCIAL MEDIA & THE INTERNET | COMPOUND WORDS

Match the compound words with their definitions.

A. bandwidth	B. download	C. firewall	D. homepage
E. keyboard	F. online	G. webcam	H. wireless

1. ________________: to be connected to the internet
2. ________________: the part of your computer used for typing letters and numbers
3. ________________: security software to protect your computer from viruses
4. ________________: technology which uses radio waves instead of cables
5. ________________: the amount of data that can be transmitted at any time
6. ________________: the first page of a website
7. ________________: to transfer data from the internet onto your computer
8. ________________: a small camera for sharing your image on the internet

SOCIAL MEDIA & THE INTERNET | SENTENCES

Use the compound words to complete the sentences.

9. There are too many cables around my desk, so I use a ________________ mouse and ________________.
10. My ________________ software is excellent at blocking viruses and pop-up ads.
11. This ________________ is very user-friendly. Everything is easy to find.
12. I post photos to my website, but people cannot ________________ them.
13. My internet connection is kind of slow. I need to increase the ________________.
14. I'm ________________ most of the day. I use my computer for everything!
15. If you want to be a Youtuber, you really need a good quality ________________.

SOCIAL MEDIA & THE INTERNET DIALOGUES

Complete the dialogues by matching the words and expressions in the box.

A. device	B. delete	C. up-to-date	D. out-of-date	E. store information
F. download	G. go online	H. do a search	I. user-friendly	J. apps

1: A: What is this little ________________?

B: It's a memory stick or thumb drive. It's used to ________________.

2: A: That report was published 20 years ago. It's ________________.

B: Oh, I see. Well, I will ________________ and ________________ for ________________ information.

3: A: She ________________ the wrong ________________. What should she do?

B: No problem. She can remove it just by clicking ________________!

4: A: I really need a new smartphone. Mine is ________________ and some ________________ don't work.

B: It still works, right? I actually think the older phones are more ________________.

SOCIAL MEDIA & THE INTERNET NAME THAT ICON

How many of these social media and internet icons can you name? Which ones do you use? Which one is your favorite? What's another one not shown here that you use frequently?

SMARTPHONE SMARTEN UP

You have 5 minutes to search for as many of the following answers as possible:

1. On average, how much time do American social media users spend online each day?
2. What is the most widely used social media platform?
3. What percent of Japanese people use social media?
4. What is the most popular messaging app in Japan?
5. Who has the most followers on Instagram?
6. How many people worldwide use social media?
7. How many videos are viewed each day on Youtube?
8. When did Twitter start?

WHO SAID THAT? FAMOUS QUOTATIONS

Talk about these quotations with your partner(s). What do you think they mean?

"The great thing about social media was how it gave a voice to voiceless people."
— Jon Ronson (journalist, Welsh, 1967-)

"It takes discipline not to let social media steal your time."
— Alexis Ohanian (internet entrepreneur, American, 1983-)

"Social media is an advertisement for the superficial extroverted self.
— Hozier (Andrew John Hozier-Byrne) (musician, Irish, 1990-)

Unit 6 Indigenous Peoples of the World

PHOTO TALK Chat freely about the photo with your partner(s). What does it tell you about today's topic?

VOCABULARY Match the words and sentences (careful of word form).

In the spaces, write: the word in Japanese / a synonym in English

A.	indigenous	/	F.	hierarchies	/
B.	industrious	/	G.	diverse	/
C.	colonized	/	H.	marginalization	/
D.	inhabit	/	I.	facing	/
E.	distinct	/	J.	ancestral	/

1. Bill is a very reliable and ______________ worker. He works a lot of overtime.
2. Britain ______________ many parts of Africa including Egypt, Zambia, and Uganda.
3. All societies have ______________. India, for example, has a caste system.
4. The forest is ______________ by many wild animals including a variety of birds.
5. The Ainu are the ______________ people of Hokkaido. They have been there for 800 years.
6. Poor people are often ______________ and not given a chance to improve their lives.
7. Japan is a small country, but it has very ______________ landscapes and weather.
8. If you don't just pay the fine, you will be ______________ a bigger problem.
9. Japanese and Chinese are very ______________ peoples. They really are very different.
10. My wife's family is from Kyushu. They have an ______________ house and farm there.

Indigenous Peoples of the World

07

1. As of 2022, there are some eight billion (8,000,000,000) people in the world. Between 370 and 500 million, or just 5% of the global population, are **indigenous** peoples living in over 90 countries. They speak more than 4,000 languages, the **vast** majority live in Asia, most are extremely poor, and their **life expectancy** is on average 20 years lower than non-indigenous people worldwide. They are proud, **industrious**, and traditional.

2. Some indigenous peoples are well known, such as the Ainu of Hokkaido, the Maya of Guatemala, the Aboriginals of Australia, and the Inuit, or Eskimo, of northern **polar** regions including Alaska, Siberia, Canada, and Greenland. Lesser-known indigenous groups include the Huli Wigmen of Papua New Guinea, the Himba of Namibia, the Cañari of Ecuador, and the Cahuilla of California.

3. *Indigenous* is from the Latin word *indigena* (from the land) and *genus* (to be born from). They are considered to be the first or native people of a land with long historical links to the region they **inhabit**, unlike colonizers or other outsiders. They **revere** ancestors and natural resources, maintain **unique** cultures, have **distinct** social **hierarchies**, and observe tradition-rooted political and religious systems. Indigenous peoples have their own languages, beliefs, and **diverse** lifestyles. **By and large**, indigenous peoples are misunderstood by **dominant** non-native groups. This **ignorance** leads to **marginalization** and **discrimination** by local people and the state.

4. Land ownership is one of the biggest challenges **facing** indigenous peoples because if they cannot control where they live, they cannot control how they live. In recent years, their rights have been increasingly recognized by local governments and at the United Nations. Indigenous people live on an **estimated** 25% of the world's land which holds 80% of the world's remaining biodiversity (e.g. rain forests and endangered species). They are guardians of nature and the environment. Despite their **ancestral** ties to a territory and its natural resources, they are usually the last to receive government investment in basic modern services such as electricity, water, and internet. They regularly **endure** inequality and **exclusion** from the general population which denies them economic, educational, and **judicial** opportunities. As a consequence, their well-being and cultures are **vulnerable**.

5. Generations of **abuse** and **injustices** have **rightly** left many indigenous groups **wary** of outsiders and their intentions. Indigenous people and their cultures are treasures that must be protected, even celebrated, rather than threatened and **criticized**. Where possible, buy their products (crafts, music, foods, etc.), promote cultural events, contribute to fundraisers, read about them, volunteer in their communities, be **compassionate** to their **plight**, and talk about them with family and friends.

Comprehension: Social Media & The Internet

Answer the Questions. Write short answers.

1. Why do you think the life expectancy of indigenous peoples is shorter than average?
2. What does the word *indigenous* mean?
3. Why is land ownership such an important issue for indigenous people?
4. Why don't indigenous peoples trust local governments?
5. What are some unique features of how indigenous people live?

Complete the Sentences. Choose the best option or options.

6. About 5% / 15% / 25% of the world's population is indigenous.
7. The life expectancy of indigenous peoples is 10 / 20 / 30 years shorter than average.
8. Indigenous peoples are proud / traditional / industrious with rich lifestyles.
9. Inequality and exclusion are / are not / typical problems for indigenous peoples.
10. Indigenous peoples are secure / protected / vulnerable in many places around the world.

True (T) or False (F). If false, correct the sentence to make it true.

11. T / F: Indigenous peoples live in over 150 countries.
12. T / F: Indigenous peoples are the first peoples of a land or nation.
13. T / F: Indigenous peoples are often the first people to receive government help.
14. T / F: The Inuit are only from Alaska.
15. T / F: Most indigenous peoples feel valued and included.

INDIGENOUS PEOPLES OF THE WORLD

Where do they live, and how big are their populations? Choose your answers.

indigenous group	*** LOCATION: region / country *** choose 1 or more			*** POPULATIONS (approximate) *** choose only 1			
Ainu	Japan	China	Russia	150,000	200,000	250,000	300,000
Inuit	Alaska	Canada	Greenland	150,000	200,700	250,000	300,000
Huli Wigmen	Malaysia	Papua New Guinea	Indonesia	51,220	150,281	201,100	250,000
Himba	Botswana	Angola	Namibia	50,400	75,625	175,000	275,625
Cañari	Ecuador	Peru	Brazil	150,450	202,890	250,000	350,000
Ndebele	South Africa	Zimbabwe	Namibia	1,202,090	2,452,072	3,002,072	4,102,054
Masai	Tanzania	Malawi	Kenya	680,777	901,888	1,200,601	1,800,553
Cherokee	USA	Canada	Mexico	130,543	230,000	300,098	351,050
Zhuang	China	Vietnam	Nepal	12,002,078	15,500,000	20,045,900	25,000,000
Sámi	Finland	Norway	Sweden	80,250	101,299	140,000	180,475
Aboriginal	Australia	New Zealand	Nauru	180,250	481,050	680,257	720,220

INDIGENOUS PEOPLES OF THE WORLD SPEAKING THEIR LANGUAGE

Many words from indigenous languages are commonly used in English (and other languages). Talk with your partner(s). How many of these words do you know? Choose 2 words you do not know, and do a quick online search about their meaning and their etymology (the origin of their meaning).

Words from Algonquian languages (speakers in Canada/USA):
These words entered English most likely via the first to meet European explorers.
Chipmunk / Eskimo / Hickory / Moccasin / Moose / Pecan / Raccoon

Words from Nahuatl (Mexico):
These words entered European languages mainly via Spanish.
Avocado / Cacao / Chocolate / Tomato

Words from Quechua (South America):
These words entered English mainly via Spanish.
Chinchilla / Jerky / Puma / Quinoa

Words from Eskimo—Aleut (Greenland, Alaska, Canada, Russia):
Anorak / Igloo / Kayak / Nanook

Words from Arawakan languages (South America):
Barbecue / Canoe / Hammock / Tobacco

Words from Tupi-Guaraní (South America)
Cashew / Capybara / Cougar / Jaguar / Tapioca

INDIGENOUS PEOPLES OF THE WORLD ASK THEM!

Imagine you are going to meet with different groups of indigenous peoples. What sorts of questions would you like to ask them? Work with your partner(s) to make a list of at least 5 questions. Examples: A. Do you have any special songs, music, or dances? What do they mean? B. What kinds of traditional foods do you eat?

YOUR QUESTIONS:

1.

2.

3.

4.

5.

6.

INDIGENOUS PEOPLES OF THE WORLD TELL THEM!

Imagine you are going to meet with different groups of indigenous peoples. What sorts of things would you like them to know about you, your culture, your life? Why do you want to share these things with them? Put your ideas on the table and the kinds of *photos* you want to share under the table. Follow the examples.

SMARTPHONE SMARTEN UP

You have 5 minutes to search for as many of the following answers as possible:

1. What is the population of the Ainu people of Hokkaido?
2. Who are the indigenous peoples of Australia?
3. Who works more, indigenous people or non-indigenous people?
4. Where do most indigenous people live — Asia, Africa, South America?
5. What is the poverty rate of native North Americans?
6. What is an "Indian reservation"?
7. How many Indian reservations are there in the United States?
8. Who is Evo Morales?

WHO SAID THAT? FAMOUS QUOTATIONS

Talk about these quotations with your partner(s). What do you think they mean?

"Although we are in different boats — you in your boat and we in our canoe — we share the same river of life."
— Oren Lyons (activist, Native American, 1930-)

"Indigenous people believe that Man belongs to the World; civilized people believe that the World belongs to Man."
— Daniel Quinn (author, American, 1935-2018)

"We are all indigenous people on this planet, and we have to reorganize to get along."
— Rebecca Adamson (writer/philosopher, Native American, 1950-)

Unit 7 Great People in History

PHOTO TALK Chat freely about the photo with your partner(s). What does it tell you about today's topic?

VOCABULARY Match the words and sentences (careful of word form).

In the spaces, write: the word in Japanese / a synonym in English

A.	intellectual	/	F.	activist	/
B.	reasoning	/	G.	assassination	/
C.	unbounded	/	H.	destitute	/
D.	issue	/	I.	charismatic	/
E.	Jews	/	J.	inordinate	/

1. After much thinking, his clear ________________ was able to solve the problem.
2. The embassy is not ________________ visas now, so I cannot go on the trip.
3. Vincent Van Gogh was a great artist, but he was ________________ when he died.
4. ________________ stand up for what they believe. Sometimes, they march in the streets.
5. Albert Einstein was a great ________________. He was a great thinker and a true genius.
6. The ________________ were murdered by the Nazis just because they were ________________.
7. The ________________ limits of space are impossible to truly understand. It's so big!
8. To be a great leader, you have to be ________________. A strong personality is important.
9. These days, I spend an ________________ amount of time using my computer.
10. The ________________ of John F. Kennedy was a shock to the United States.

Read All About It

08

Great People in History

1. Throughout history, great people from each **generation** shape and influence the world. They include scientists, religious figures, politicians, military leaders, philosophers, musicians, artists, and inventors. Who are these people, and what makes them great?

2. Aristotle (384 BC-322 BC, Greek) was a philosopher and scientist. His **intellectual** insights included biology, chemistry, logic, physics, political theory, and psychology. He was the first to use scientific and factual **reasoning** in the study of nature.

3. Leonardo da Vinci (1452-1519, Italian) was much more than a painter. He was an inventor, scientist, engineer, theorist, anatomist, and architect. He also had great knowledge in astronomy, botany, and cartography. His **genius** was **unbounded**.

4. Sir Isaac Newton (1643-1727, English) was a mathematician, physicist, astronomer, and theologian who is best-known for inventing calculus, his theories of universal **gravity**, and his three laws of motion. He changed our understanding of the universe.

5. Chiune Sugihara (1900-1986, Japanese) was a **diplomat** who was **vice-consul** for the Japanese Empire in Kaunas, Lithuania during World War II. At great risk to himself and his family, he **issued** life-saving transit visas to some 2,000 **Jews**. In 1985, the State of Israel honored him as one of the Righteous Among the Nations.

6. Mother Teresa (1910-1997, Albanian) was a Catholic nun who dedicated her life to caring for the **destitute** in Kolkata, India. She won the Nobel Peace Prize in 1979.

7. Martin Luther King, Jr. (1929-1968, American) was a Baptist **minister** and **activist** who spearheaded the Civil Rights Movement until his **assassination**. A great writer, thinker, and **orator**, he is most famous for his "I Have a Dream" speech given on August 28, 1963.

8. Great people share many similar characteristics. They are **charismatic** and endlessly **curious**. They are **avid** readers and big dreamers. They are excellent communicators and even better listeners. They are **boldly** confident yet **humble** and are not afraid of failure. They take responsibility and do not **blame** others. They **think outside the box** and take risks. They work hard but know how to have fun. They believe in their vision and know how to **adapt**. They are willing to try things beyond their **comfort zone** and are willing to be **embarrassed**. They make mistakes and learn from them. They have **inordinate** energy and good thinking skills. They inspire and value other people.

9. Everyone is born with the **potential** to be a great influencer, leader, and thinker. Do you have what it takes to be the change you want to see in the world?

Comprehension: Great People in History

Answer the Questions. Write short answers.

1. What kinds of people are "great people of the world"?
2. Leonardo da Vinci was not just a painter. What else is he known for?
3. What is one thing Sir Isaac Newton did?
4. Who was Chiune Sugihara?
5. What kind of personality do many great people have?

Complete the Sentences. Choose the best option or options.

6. Chiune Sugihara save the lives of about 2,000 / 12,000 / 20,000 Jews from the Nazis.
7. Martin Luther King Jr. was a/an minister / activist / civil rights leader.
8. Great people have quiet / private / charismatic personalities.
9. Aristotle was a Roman / Greek / Italian philosopher.
10. Mother Teresa was an Indian / Albanian / Italian nun who helped the poor.

True (T) or False (F). If false, correct the sentence to make it true.

11. T / F: The speech "I Have a Dream" was given by Martin Luther King Jr.
12. T / F: Not everyone has the potential to be a great leader.
13. T / F: Chiune Sugihara worked in Latvia during World War II.
14. T / F: To "think outside the box" means to think differently about something.
15. T / F: Great leaders know how to work hard and how to have fun too.

GREAT PEOPLE IN HISTORY YESTERDAY AND TODAY

STEP 1: Circle the numbers of the people on this chart that you know. Then, with your partner(s), complete the chart as best as you can.

STEP 2: All of these people are famous, but which ones do you think are really great? Why? What makes them great? Write a list of ideas. What did/do they contribute to the world that makes them great? Think about some of the points in the reading, especially the part about characteristics of great people.

STEP 3: If you could meet only one of the people on this list, who would it be and why? What would you like to ask or tell them? Use your smartphone to find a photo of this person, and talk to them!

STEP 4: Add 1~3 great names to the list and explain to your partner(s) what you think makes these people great.

	NAME	LIVING / DEAD	NATIONALITY	FAMOUS FOR
1.	Paul McCartney			
2.	Audrey Hepburn			
3.	Greta Thunberg			
4.	Bill Gates			
5.	Hayao Miyazaki			
6.	Coco Chanel			
7.	Malala Yousafzai			
8.	Nelson Mandela			
9.	Helen Keller			
10.	Ichiro Suzuki			
11.	J.K. Rowling			
12.	Marie Curie			
13.	Albert Einstein			
14.				
15.				

GREAT PEOPLE IN HISTORY GREAT PEOPLE IN MY LIFE

In the previous activity, you discussed famous great people in history. Now it's time to think about the great people in your life. Not every great person is famous, and not every famous person is great. Some of our biggest heroes are the people we know and love — family members, friends, teachers, colleagues, acquaintances.

Think of 1~2 people you know personally whom you think are great. What makes them great? Complete the chart below with some key words about them and a few words about how they make you feel.

__________________ is a great person in my life.

WHAT MAKES THEM GREAT:

HOW THEY MAKE ME FEEL:

__________________ is a great person in my life.

WHAT MAKES THEM GREAT:

HOW THEY MAKE ME FEEL:

GREAT PEOPLE IN HISTORY BEING A GREAT PERSON

Would you like to be known and remembered for being a great person in history? If yes, for what? If no, what's another way you would like to be remembered. Complete the sentences below and then share with your partner(s).

I would like to be a famous great person for __________________.
In order to achieve greatness, I must __________________ and __________________.
I think being a great person means __________________.
But I don't think being great is someone who __________________.
A great person has / does not have __________________. I think being a famous great person would be fun / challenging / a big responsibility because __________________. As a great person, my goals would be to __________________, __________________, and __________________. I hope people will think I am a __________________ person. But most of all, I think __________________.

SMARTPHONE SMARTEN UP

You have 5 minutes to search for as many of the following answers as possible:

1. Who was Genghis Khan?
2. Who was William Shakespeare?
3. Who was Anne Frank?
4. Who was Johannes Gutenberg?
5. Who was Oda Nobunaga?
6. Who was Anne Boleyn?
7. Who was Karl Marx?
8. Who was John Lennon?

WHO SAID THAT? FAMOUS QUOTATIONS

Talk about these quotations with your partner(s). What do you think they mean?

"I want to work with great people. Great people really make you better."
— Dennis Quaid (actor, American, 1954-)

"Great countries are those that produce great people."
— Benjamin Disraeli (politician, British, 1804-1881)

"You want to be great? Help others achieve their greatness."
— Bangambiki Habyarimana (writer, Rwandan, dob. ?)

Unit 8 The Road Less (or More) Traveled

PHOTO TALK Chat freely about the photo with your partner(s). What does it tell you about today's topic?

VOCABULARY Match the words and sentences (careful of word form).

In the spaces, write: the word in Japanese / a synonym in English

A.	yearn	/	F.	serendipitous	/
B.	leisure	/	G.	literally	/
C.	traverse	/	H.	perspective	/
D.	migration	/	I.	marvel	/
E.	surrender	/	J.	urgency	/

1. The hike is long and tough. We have to ______________ two rivers and a mountain.
2. The Grand Canyon is one of the greatest ______________ to see at least once in your life!
3. Never ______________ your dreams, or you will regret it later!
4. The name of the cheese is Dolcelatte, ______________ meaning 'sweet milk'.
5. Each year, more and more people are traveling for ______________ rather than for business.
6. My friend and I had a ______________ meeting in Paris. It was so much fun!
7. Travel helps you to change your life ______________ and to have an open mind.
8. There was an ______________ to get to the embassy before it closed for the day.
9. Every year, birds and other animals ______________ thousands of kilometers.
10. Overseas travel always makes me ______________ for the comforts of home.

Read All About It

09

The Road Less (or More) Traveled

1. Since time **immemorial**, mankind has **yearned** to travel. The earliest-known people **ventured** from their homes to hunt for food and gather materials. In **antiquity** (1000 BC-450 CE), Greeks and Romans traveled for **leisure**. During the Age of Exploration (c.1400-1900), Europeans — mainly the Portuguese, Spanish, Dutch, and English — **traversed** the world in search of riches in trade, to **conquer** new lands, and to spread their religion. In modern times, however, travel is primarily associated with holidays. Other reasons for travel include business, health and relaxation, discovery and exploration, **migration**, religious pilgrimages, relationships, adventure, and a sense of freedom.

2. People travel to lose themselves, to **surrender** the familiar things of home only to discover something new within their **souls**. Travel is a great teacher, and learning, therefore, is a **compelling** reason to travel. New and unique experiences open our eyes, minds, and hearts to different cultures and lifestyles. Some journeys are wandering, **serendipitous**, and without specific plans. Others are taken to learn something particular such as a language, dance, yoga, history, or about the natural world.

3. Travel is about discovery and exploration, sometimes **literally**, but more often self-discovery and exploring an unfamiliar place. Experiencing different cultures opens our eyes to our own cultures too. More than simply trying new foods, we can taste the different spices of life the world has to offer. Travel expands our **horizons** and **perspective**. By discovering new places and meeting local people, you realize there are many ways to live, love, and laugh. Travel shows us that the world is far safer than it appears on TV, and that the majority of people are good, helpful, and welcoming. No books, films, or classrooms can **substitute** for such experiences.

4. Though the world is full of beauty and **marvel**, travel at times reveals ugly realities of life of less fortunate souls. **Poverty**, for instance, is **rife** in many countries, even the **wealthiest** nations. Travel reveals the world's **inequities**, the **moral** and political **urgencies**, and life-and-death circumstances we typically do not face at home.

5. Travel will change you. It will reward you with fresh ideas, possibilities, memories, stories, and creativity. Your **encounters** will **enrich** your understanding of and **compassion** for your fellow human beings by widening your worldview. Travel is a mirror on your own life, home, and culture because it **reflects** who you are and what you and your culture offer visitors.

6. If you can travel, you are a lucky person. Most people will never have the opportunity because they do not have the time or they are **forbidden** to do so by either their family, culture, circumstances, or government.

Comprehension: The Road Less (or More) Traveled

Answer the Questions. Write short answers.

1. Why did the earliest peoples travel?
2. What does it mean to "lose yourself" while traveling?
3. Why did early European explorers travel the world?
4. Why are you "lucky" if you can travel?
5. What are some benefits of travel?

Complete the Sentences. Choose the best option or options.

6. Ancient Greeks and Romans traveled for food / work / leisure.
7. The European Age of Exploration was from about 600~900 / 1000~1200 / 1400~1900.
8. Travel is sometimes serendipitous / planned / without specific plans.
9. Travel shows us that the world is safer / more dangerous / scarier than it is on TV.
10. Most people in the world are good / unwelcoming / not friendly.

True (T) or False (F). If false, correct the sentence to make it true.

11. T / F: During the Age of Exploration, Europeans wanted to conquer other lands.
12. T / F: Travel experiences help people open their minds to new cultures and ways of life.
13. T / F: Travel is like a mirror because it reflects things about your own culture.
14. T / F: Everyone has the freedom to travel, but not everyone has the money or time.
15. T / F: The Age of Exploration was a peaceful period of cultural exchange.

THE ROAD LESS TRAVELED | TRAVEL PHOTOS & EXPERIENCES

Look at the photos with your partner(s) and discuss them. Imagine you are in each of these places. What does each destination offer visitors? What can travelers see and do?

Laguna Polques, Bolivia

New York City, USA

Ayuthaya, Thailand

Oslo, Norway

Hanoi, Vietnam

Tokyo, Japan

THE ROAD LESS TRAVELED
SHARE A TRAVEL MEMORY

Choose 1 travel photo on your smartphone. It can be from an overseas trip or one here in Japan — but it should be a travel photo, not one from a normal day.

Describe what makes this photo and this travel experience worth sharing. Convince your partner(s) why they should or should not go there.

THE ROAD LESS TRAVELED TRAVEL QUIZ

Discuss these travel questions with your partner(s). However, you do not have to select the same answers. Then, count up your total correct answers.

1. **How many U.S. states are there?**
   A. 48 B. 50 C. 52
2. **What is the capital city of Australia?**
   A. Canberra B. Sydney C. Adelaide
3. **Where is the Eiffel Tower?**
   A. Brussels, Belgium B. Paris, France C. London, England
4. **What river flows through London, England?**
   A. The Seine B. The Thames C. The Rhine
5. **Where are the Pyramids of Egypt?**
   A. Cairo B. Luxor C. Giza
6. **How many countries are there in South America?**
   A. 10 B. 12 C. 15
7. **Which is the most populated continent?**
   A. Asia B. Africa C. Europe
8. **What is the second longest river in the world?**
   A. The Amazon (Brazil) B. The Nile (Egypt) C. The Yangtze (China)
9. **Where is the lowest place on Earth?**
   A. The Dead Sea (Israel/Jordan) B. Lake Assad (Djibouti) C. Death Valley (USA)
10. **Which is the world's largest desert?**
    A. Arabian Desert B. Antarctic Desert C. Sahara Desert
11. **Where is Big Ben (and what is it)?**
    A. London, England B. Rome, Italy C. New York, USA
12. **Where is Uluru, also known as Ayer's Rock?**
    A. Australia B. New Zealand C. Indonesia
13. **Which South American country is known for Carnival?**
    A. Argentina B. Chile C. Brazil
14. **Which African country is home to lemur monkeys?**
    A. South Africa B. Zimbabwe C. Madagascar
15. **Where is Machu Picchu?**
    A. Bolivia B. Peru C. Ecuador
16. **Which U.S. city is famous for jazz music?**
    A. New York City B. New Orleans C. Boston
17. **What is your religion if you pray towards Mecca?**
    A. Islam B. Judaism C. Christianity
18. **Which Asian nation is famous for horses?**
    A. Nepal B. Mongolia C. Bhutan
19. **What is the world's most populated island nation?**
    A. Indonesia B. Japan C. Sri Lanka
20. **What does "stan" mean, as in Pakistan and Afghanistan?**
    A. Country B. Land C. Mountains

TIE BREAKER: How many islands does Japan have?
A. 4 B. 129 C. 6,852

TOTAL CORRECT ANSWERS: _____ / 20

SMARTPHONE SMARTEN UP

You have 5 minutes to search for as many of the following answers as possible:

1. What is 2nd largest country in the world by size (not population)?
2. What is the currency of Poland?
3. If you are flying to LAX, where are you going?
4. What is the name of the train that goes between London and Paris?
5. What country controls the Galapagos Islands?
6. What is the most populated country in Africa?
7. How do you say hello in French?
8. Which country has the most languages?

WHO SAID THAT? FAMOUS QUOTATIONS

Talk about these quotations with your partner(s). What do you think they mean?

"The world is a book, and those who do not travel read only one page."
— Saint Augustine of Hippo (philosopher, Algerian, 354-430)

"To travel is to live."
— Hans Christian Andersen (author, Danish, 1805-1875)

"You go away for a long time and return a different person – you never come all the way back."
— Paul Theroux (writer, American, 1941-)

Unit 9 The Culture of Food

PHOTO TALK Chat freely about the photo with your partner(s). What does it tell you about today's topic?

VOCABULARY **Match the words and sentences (careful of word form).**

In the spaces, write: the word in Japanese / a synonym in English

A.	substance	/	F.	ingredients	/
B.	nutrition	/	G.	intertwined	/
C.	sustenance	/	H.	culinary	/
D.	forge	/	I.	ready-made	/
E.	aspiration	/	J.	obesity	/

1. Good ________________ requires eating fresh fruits and vegetables every day.
2. My sister has never had much ________________ to earn a lot of money.
3. Traveling alone ________________ new friendships because you have to talk to strangers.
4. Some foods are simple to cook, but others require a lot of ________________.
5. Even as a boy, John was fat. Now, his ________________ is out of control. It's very sad.
6. Water is the most important ________________ in the world. Without it, there is no life.
7. The world is more and more ________________ as internet and social media spread.
8. Stacey attended ________________ school in France for 3 years. Now she's a top chef!
9. I don't like ________________ meals. I prefer to cook a fresh and healthy meal.
10. The villagers depend on the sea for ________________. They eat fish at each meal.

The Culture of Food

10

1. Food is any **substance** that people or animals eat or drink for **nutrition**. In all nations and communities, food is at the very center of daily life not only for **sustenance**, but for social connections, events, celebrations, cultural identity and exchange. It is impossible to imagine social activities without food or drinks or welcoming a guest to one's home and not offering a **refreshment**. Food is a unifier that can **forge** new friendships and be presented as offerings of peace or love. It represents status, power, wealth, **hospitality**, and tradition and symbolizes a range of emotions and **aspirations**. Food — its smells and flavors — **bonds** us to memories and transports us to other cultures.

2. Food culture refers to attitudes, customs, and beliefs about food, as well as preparation methods and consumption etiquette. These **attributes** vary by country, region, and ethnic group. Yet, food cultures can vary greatly within regions depending upon how the **ingredients** are prepared. It is also about the environment, the availability of ingredients, and how we experience the food. Some food cultures are globally **distinctive** while many remain local specialties. But for all their differences, food cultures undeniably share two **traits**: community and pleasure. Sharing a meal with someone is a joy.

3. Food and culture are **intertwined**. In fact, UNESCO has **designated** a number of cuisines as cultural treasures, including traditional French and Mexican dishes, Neapolitan pizza, Turkish coffee, Belgian beers, and Japanese washoku. For travelers getting to know a place, **culinary** traditions are a **vital** source of learning and experiencing.

4. **Despite** the long and tasty history of food culture, the **foodie** was born in the 1980s when the word was first used in an article in New York Magazine. A foodie is a person who has a passionate or **refined** interest in food and who eats not only when hungry, but for a hobby, follows food trends, and takes pleasure from cooking and talking about food.

5. In the 2000s, foodie trends rapidly increased through social media and the ease of international travel. But commercially processed **packaged** foods and big supermarket chains have **detached** many cultures from their traditional foods, particularly in the United States, as pre-cooked, frozen, and **ready-made** meals became popular. The health impacts **manifest** in rising numbers of **obesity** worldwide.

6. Food culture starts in your kitchen, not at a **trendy** restaurant. Create and **maintain** your local food culture by cooking dishes you love and the ones your parents and grandparents used to make. Find and use local **ingredients**. Change flavors and recipes with the seasons. Above all, respect and **appreciate** the food you eat — there are millions of hungry people around the world who would be **delighted** to share your table.

Comprehension: Social Media & The Internet

Answer the Questions. Write short answers.

1. Besides nutrition, how else is food important in each culture?
2. What does "food culture" mean?
3. What are some examples of foods UNESCO considers cultural treasures?
4. What is a foodie?
5. Where does food culture begin?

Complete the Sentences. Choose the best option or options.

6. Ready-made foods are increasing / decreasing / not changing rates of obesity.
7. Food is important for health / community / memories.
8. Food and culture are intertwined / separate / unrelated aspects of society.
9. Experiencing culinary specialities is important to business people / tourists / friends.
10. The term "foodie" has been around since the 1960s / 1970s / 1980s.

True (T) or False (F). If false, correct the sentence to make it true.

11. T / F: A foodie likes to eat at lots of restaurants, but they don't like to cook very often.
12. T / F: UNESCO has recognized many national dishes and drinks as cultural treasures.
13. T / F: Sharing a meal or drink with someone is a universal gesture of welcome.
14. T / F: The smell of some foods reminds us of childhood memories.
15. T / F: Food etiquette is generally the same worldwide, but attitudes are different.

THE CULTURE OF FOOD DESCRIBING FOOD

Food can be described in many ways including its appearance, the ingredients, how it's prepared, and how it tastes. You can also describe how and when it's eaten — daily or for special occasions. With your partner(s), read these food descriptions. What are they? When you finish, take turns describing some of the foods in the box. Follow the examples.

1. It's a thick, white drink. Similar to nihonshu (sake), it's made from fermented rice but it is very low in alcohol. It is sweet, usually served hot, and popular at New Year.

2. It's a kind of round flat bread covered with tomato sauce. It is topped with cheese and slices of sausage or vegetables. Some people even like to put fruit on it. It is baked.

3. It has 2 slices of bread or toast covered with mayonnaise, butter, or mustard. Popular fillings include egg, ham, tuna, or chicken and lettuce or sliced tomatoes. It is eaten with your hands.

4. This dish is a kind of porridge made from seven spring herbs. It is eaten on January 7. Eating it is supposed to help you live a long life.

5. This dish is made with sliced eel grilled in a thick sweet barbecue sauce. It is usually served hot over a bowl of rice. It's most popular in summer.

Now try describing some of these foods — and your favorite dish!

sushi hamburgers fish and chips ice cream ramen
tempura miso soup salad spaghetti with meatballs
okonomiyaki onigiri chocolate cake quiche croquette

THE CULTURE OF FOOD EATING ETIQUETTE AROUND THE WORLD

Choose the best answer.

1. In India, always eat with your left / right hand.
2. In France, don't eat / eat all the bread before your food.
3. In Egypt, wait / don't wait for someone else to refill your glass.
4. In Italy, add / don't add extra condiments (toppings) to your pizza.
5. In Japan, it is ok / not ok to tip in restaurants.
6. In Korea, receive a plate of food with the left hand / the right hand / both hands.
7. In China, eat a fish from only one side / from both sides.
8. In Thailand, don't use / use a fork to put food into your mouth.
9. In Chile, it's ok / not ok to eat with your hands.
10. In Kazakhstan, a full cup / half a cup of tea means the host likes you.
11. In Portugal, do / don't ask for salt and pepper.
12. In Taiwan, burping is / is not considered a compliment to the chef.

THE CULTURE OF FOOD DINING IN A UNIQUE RESTAURANT

One student is **The Server**, and one student is **The Guest**.

STEP 1: Unjumble the conversation (only look at your part). **STEP 2:** Read the whole conversation together. **STEP 3:** Replace all of the underlined words with your own fun and funky ideas. **STEP 4:** Read it again with a different partner.

~ THE SERVER ~

___ Today's soups are cream of apple and elbow noodle.
(fruit) (body part)

___ Outstanding. Both are crazy yummy. How about something to drink?
(adjective) (taste adjective)

7 I'm sure the chef can make that for you. How about the main course?

___ I'll place your order now. You are going to have a disgusting dinner! Enjoy!
(adjective)

___ Fine choice. Would you like some chocolate with that?
(snack food)

___ Welcome to the Unique Restaurant. My name is Starving. I'm your server.
(adjective) (emotion word)

3 Certainly. Would you like them hot and spicy?
(adjective) (flavor)

___ Absolutely. For dessert, how about sunflower cake or crab ice cream?
(a flower) (seafood)

___ I will bring that with our compliments. How about a butterfly salad?
(insect)

___ Would you like to try some cheese in that?
(a refrigerator food)

~ THE GUEST ~

___ Of course! I'd like 13 pieces of cake and 101 scoops of ice cream.
(number) (number)

___ Yeah, that sounds tasty. Is there a soup of the day?
(taste adjective)

___ Well, the bloody zebra chop sounds really gross. I'll have that, please.
(adjective) (animal) (adjective)

___ No, thank you. I think that's enough for this evening.

___ Fantastic! It all sounds horrible. I can't wait!
(adjective) (adjective)

2 Thank you. For my starter, I'd like a plate of boiled ants.
(insect)

___ By any chance, do you have hamster tail soup?
(pet) (body part)

12 Oh, yes. I love salad. Please put some milk dressing on it.
(drink)

___ No, thank you. But I'd like some black cabbage bread.
(color) (vegetable)

___ Please bring me a running mug of honey.
(-ing verb) (liquid)

SMARTPHONE SMARTEN UP

You have 5 minutes to search for as many of the following answers as possible:

1. What is a national main dish of Thailand?
2. Tagine (pron. ta-jeen) is a slow cooked stew famous in what country?
3. What is a national main dish of South Africa?
4. In which southeast Asian nation are pho (noodles) popular?
5. What is a national main dish of Australia?
6. Fish and chips is a popular dish in which European country?
7. Where can you eat pot-au-feu (a hearty stew)?
8. Hákarl (shark) is a national main dish of which Scandinavian country?

WHO SAID THAT? FAMOUS QUOTATIONS

Talk about these quotations with your partner(s). What do you think they mean?

"All you need is love. But a little chocolate now and then doesn't hurt."
— Charles M. Schulz (cartoonist, American, 1922-2000)

"There are people in the world so hungry, that God cannot appear to them except in the form of bread."
— Mahatma Gandhi (lawyer/activist, Indian, 1869-1948)

"There is no love sincerer than the love of food."
— George Bernard Shaw (writer/political activist, Irish, 1856-1950)

Unit 10 Freedom and Responsibility

PHOTO TALK Chat freely about the photo with your partner(s). What does it tell you about today's topic?

VOCABULARY Match the words and sentences (careful of word form).

In the spaces, write: the word in Japanese / a synonym in English

A.	autonomy	/	F.	outcome	/
B.	constrained	/	G.	oppression	/
C.	defame	/	H.	authority	/
D.	presuppose	/	I.	limitation	/
E.	restraint	/	J.	probable cause	/

1. Women have always been ______________ by men and their power, but times are changing!
2. If I see chocolate, I have to eat it. I just cannot ______________ myself.
3. If there were no ______________ on freedom, society would be disorganized and scary.
4. The ______________ of the case will not be decided before the end of the year.
5. The police cannot arrest someone without ______________. There must be a reason.
6. Your opinion ______________ that the facts are wrong, but facts are facts.
7. Japan is a free country, but many governments ______________ their people.
8. The government has the ______________ to make laws and rules.
9. Teenagers should have the ______________ to make their own decisions.
10. Politicians often ______________ each other, especially during election time.

Read All About It

Freedom and Responsibility

11

1. *Freedom* is the power of choice and control over our actions and decisions. In philosophy, this **autonomy** is called **free will**. *Responsibility* is a person's accountability for their actions. People are responsible for their free actions. Freedom and responsibility are **entwined**; one cannot exist without the other. Freedom is not **absolute** and is **constrained** by responsibility (you cannot yell "fire!" in a theater or **defame** someone). Responsibility, on the other hand, **presupposes** that an individual is free to make their own decisions based on one's own **conscience**, **morals**, and **values**. Freedom without responsibility would lead to **chaos** because there would be no **restraints** or limitations on **behavior**. Freedom is **regulated** by factors that **vary** by country and community including social norms, morals, values, customs, laws, rules, fear, or violence.

2. The expression "to take responsibility for your actions" means **admitting** one's freedom of actions resulted in a negative outcome. By "taking responsibility", you express an **ownership** of your behavior. Free actions and words have consequences, often times positive, but sometimes negative. Taking responsibility for our actions means **acknowledging** those actions and accepting the **outcomes**, particularly when they are negative, hurtful, or unlawful. Taking responsibility means not **blaming** others and **apologizing** when necessary. By taking responsibility, wrongs can sometimes be righted. Taking responsibility is a **vital** aspect of relationships, and it makes you a good **citizen**.

3. The **terms** freedom and liberty are used **interchangeably**, but they actually mean different things. Freedom is ownership of what goes on inside our heads (our thoughts) and hearts (our desires and dreams). So, for example, our freedom of movement (our liberty) can be taken away, but our freedom to think cannot. To have liberty, therefore, is to live in a society free of **oppression** on our way of life by an **authority** (e.g. a government, a religious **sect**, or cultural customs).

4. Freedom is **measured** in many ways including politically, socially, and economically. Political freedom is freedom from oppression by a government. **Civil rights** include freedom of thought, religion, expression, speech, and movement. Economic freedom is the ability to control one's property, labor, and to build personal wealth. In 2021, New Zealand ranked as the world's freest country, Japan 25th, and Syria the least.

5. All societies have **limitations** on freedom. Everyone everywhere has social responsibilities under the law, for example, to pay taxes, to educate their children, and to obey traffic laws. Professional responsibilities require following **codes of conduct**, for example, police officers cannot arrest people without **probable cause**. Moral, or personal, responsibility is perhaps the most important of all because it makes us human and gives us a conscience to be compassionate, considerate, and caring.

Comprehension: Freedom and Responsibility

Answer the Questions. Write short answers.

1. What is freedom and free will?
2. What is an example of a constraint on freedom?
3. What does it mean to "take responsibility for your actions"?
4. What is the difference between freedom and liberty?
5. What are some examples of civil rights?

Complete the Sentences. Choose the best option or options.

6. Freedom is measured the same / differently / fairly in each country.
7. The police cannot arrest a person without permission / probable cause / a witness.
8. Freedom is determined by governments / laws / culture.
9. New Zealand / Australia / America ranked as the freest country in 2021.
10. All / some / most nations and societies have limitations on freedom.

True (T) or False (F). If false, correct the sentence to make it true.

11. T / F: Not all countries and societies have limitations on freedom.
12. T / F: Freedoms vary in each country.
13. T / F: An example of liberty is the freedom to travel.
14. T / F: Moral responsibility gives humans a conscience and limits our actions.
15. T / F: Blaming others is a good way to take responsibility for our actions.

FREEDOM AND RESPONSIBILITY ASK IT > ANSWER IT

Work with your partner(s) to ask and answer the questions below. Feel free to ask some of your own questions about freedom.

GENERAL QUESTIONS:

1. How free do you feel from 0% to 100%? Explain your answer with examples.
2. What is a country you think is not free? Why do you think it is not free? Explain.
3. What comes to your mind when you hear the word "freedom"?
4. Was there a time that you did not feel free to choose something? What was it?
5. Who or what is a symbol of freedom to you (in Japan or the world)?
6. Do you believe in complete freedom?
7. Many governments censor (control/limit) internet/TV/news. Should this be allowed?

SITUATION QUESTIONS:

8. Do you think it is ok for the government to limit freedoms – for example, freedom of speech – if doing so will make you and society safer?
9. A Muslim university student is linked to a terrorist group. Should the police be allowed to monitor Muslim student associations for terrorist activity?
10. The government orders a technology company to unlock a phone it manufactures for an investigation. Should this be allowed?
11. The police stop you because you "look suspicious". Should this be allowed?
12. An anti-LGBTQ group is on a public sidewalk in front of a school shouting anti-gay slurs as students arrive for classes. Should this be allowed?

FREEDOM AND RESPONSIBILITY THE UNITED NATIONS

Human Rights are an important aspect of freedom. In 1948, the United Nations adopted the *Universal Declaration of Human Rights*. It features 30 Articles, or sections. The following list includes only some of these Rights. Talk with your partner(s) about them. Do you think these apply in Japan (or your country)? Even if your answer is yes or no, explain with examples, reasons, or personal experiences.

ARTICLE 1: All human beings are born free and equal in dignity and rights.
ARTICLE 3: Everyone has the right to life, liberty and the security of person.
ARTICLE 4: No one shall be held in slavery or servitude.
ARTICLE 5: No one shall be subjected to torture or to cruel, inhuman or degrading treatment or punishment.
ARTICLE 7: All are equal before the law and are entitled without any discrimination to equal protection of the law.
ARTICLE 9: No one shall be subjected to arbitrary arrest, detention or exile.
ARTICLE 12: No one shall be subjected to arbitrary interference with his privacy, family, home or correspondence.
ARTICLE 14: Everyone has the right to seek asylum from persecution.
ARTICLE 15: Everyone has the right to a nationality.
ARTICLE 17: Everyone has the right to own property.
ARTICLE 19: Everyone has the right to freedom of opinion and expression.
ARTICLE 26: Everyone has the right to education.

FREEDOM AND RESPONSIBILITY | MY OWN

Each one of us yearns to be free. But each one of us also has responsibilities to ourselves, our families, our friends, our jobs, our fellow citizens. None of us live in complete freedom. We are bound by rules and laws, customs and traditions, and social manners. Take a few minutes to think about what makes you feel free and what your responsibilities are. Makes notes in the spaces below. Then, talk freely with your partner(s). What seems to be similar or different between you? Explain.

MY FREEDOMS

Things that make me feel free:

ON MY OWN:	WITH OTHER PEOPLE:
listening to music	karaoke

MY RESPONSIBILITIES

Things that I am responsible for:

FOR MYSELF:	FOR OTHER PEOPLE:
doing my homework	cleaning the house

SMARTPHONE SMARTEN UP

You have 5 minutes to search for as many of the following answers as possible:

1. What does the Statue of Liberty symbolize, and where is it?
2. What white bird is a universal symbol of freedom and peace?
3. How do national flags symbolize freedom?
4. How do you say "freedom" in French?
5. What is the Phrygian cap?
6. In what country is the Bald Eagle a symbol of freedom and liberty?
7. Where is the Liberty Bell?
8. In what religion are golden fish a symbol of freedom of movement?

WHO SAID THAT? FAMOUS QUOTATIONS

Talk about these quotations with your partner(s). What do you think they mean?

"Responsibility is the price of freedom."
— Elbert Hubbard (writer/philosopher, American, 1856-1915)

"Give me liberty, or give me death."
— Patrick Henry (politician, American, 1736-1799)

"Life without freedom is like a body without spirit."
— Kahlil Gibran (writer, Lebanese, 1883-1931)

Unit 11 Love One, Love All

PHOTO TALK Chat freely about the photo with your partner(s). What does it tell you about today's topic?

VOCABULARY Match the words and sentences (careful of word form).

In the spaces, write: the word in Japanese / a synonym in English

A.	intense	/	F.	courtship	/
B.	primal	/	G.	attract	/
C.	by whatever means	/	H.	emblematic	/
D.	contain	/	I.	abdicate	/
E.	convey	/	J.	splendor	/

1. Whenever I smell bacon, I have a ______________ desire to eat my mother's cooking.
2. I cannot ______________ my feelings in words, so I bought you this gift to thank you.
3. ______________, you will have to pay me back by the end of the week. I need the money.
4. They only had a 6-month ______________ before they got married. I think it's too soon.
5. The people were amazed at the ______________ of the queen's jewelry and tiara.
6. The kimono is ______________ of Japanese beauty, a symbol known all over the world.
7. People want to look good in order to ______________ a partner. That's normal behavior.
8. Bill agreed to ______________ and retire so his son could take control of the company.
9. The flood could not be ______________. The entire city was damaged.
10. Nigel and Pam had an ______________ love, but after a few years, they broke up.

12

Love One, Love All

1. Love is **intense** positive emotional, mental, and physical feelings. Love ranges from romantic to **familial**, from love of friends to love of things and experiences. Love is associated with kindness, affection, compassion, and empathy. Love is a **primal** human feeling. Love is universal but **manifests** in different ways. Culture, customs, and religion impact our notions of love and the way we feel, think, and **behave** in romantic relationships. Love, in all its forms, is essential for a fulfilling life. Love is a foundation of human existence, for without it, the **species** may die.

2. In English, the word love can be **applied** to any situation, from "I love you" to "I love sushi." In Japanese, "suki (to like)" is more commonly used than "ai (love)". Sanskrit, spoken in India, has 96 words for love. Yet, Ilocano, spoken in the Philippines, has no word for love. Some cultures, such as French, express love **explicitly** in words while others, as the Japanese, do so **implicitly** through actions. **By whatever means**, since ancient times, Eros and Cupid, the Greek and Roman gods of love, **respectively**, have symbolized romance and passion. Throughout the ages, love has been at the heart of the **creative arts** because love cannot be **contained**. Even without words, love is felt, shared, and **conveyed** between a couple, a parent and child, or friends.

3. It is hardly surprising that love is expressed differently around the world. In the United States, it is usual for men to give women a card and chocolates on Valentine's Day. Zulu girls of South Africa express their love by making love letters out of colorful beads. The colors represent different feelings. In Fiji, a man presents a **whale** tooth to the father of the woman he loves in the hopes of marrying her. In South Korea, the 14th of every month celebrates a different love theme, for example, Kiss Day (June) and Photo Day (September). In Germany, pig-themed gifts are given to symbolize good fortune and love. In Niger, males participate in an annual **courtship** called Guérewol in which they wear special costumes and makeup and perform a traditional dance in order to **attract** a lover.

4. There are many great love stories throughout history, some fictional, some real. Perhaps the most famous lovers of all time are Mark Antony, a Roman General, and Cleopatra, the Queen of Egypt. Their story has been told for two **millennia**. In **literature**, the romance of Romeo and Juliet has been **emblematic** of love ever since Shakespeare wrote the story in 1595. In 1936, King Edward VIII of the UK **abdicated** the **throne** for the love of his life, Wallis Simpson. Other great loves include Anne Boleyn and Henry VIII, artists Diego Rivera and Frida Kahlo, Grace Kelly and Prince Rainier of Monaco, John Lennon and Yoko Ono. In Japan, each July 7, Tanabata Festival celebrates the annual **reunion** between Vega and Altair, two lovers in the Milky Way.

5. In any culture and at any point in history, love is a many-splendored thing.

Comprehension: Love One, Love All

Answer the Questions. Write short answers.

1. What is love?
2. What does "love is a primal human feeling" mean?
3. What are some cultural differences in how people express love?
4. Why is love a major theme of the creative arts?
5. Why do you think some cultures express love more and less directly?

Complete the Sentences. Choose the best option or options.

6. In Fiji, a man presents a <u>whale tooth</u> / <u>turtle shell</u> / <u>dolphin bone</u> to his bride's father.
7. Love is the foundation of human <u>joy</u> / <u>culture</u> / <u>existence</u>.
8. Cupid is the <u>Greek</u> / <u>Roman</u> / <u>Italian</u> god of love.
9. In Germany, pig-themed gifts symbolize <u>good fortune</u> / <u>desire</u> / <u>gratitude</u>.
10. The love story of Antony and Cleopatra is <u>1,000</u> / <u>2,000</u> / <u>3,000</u> years old.

True (T) or False (F). If false, correct the sentence to make it true.

11. T / F: King Edward VIII divorced Wallis Simpson in order to remain king.
12. T / F: In South Korea, young couples celebrate Valentine's Day once a year.
13. T / F: Without love, the human species may die.
14. T / F: Some cultures express love through actions more than words.
15. T / F: In English, the word *love* is used to describe almost anything someone really likes.

LOVE ONE, LOVE ALL | LOVE SURVEY

PART A: You are going to ask only one of these questions to as many classmates as possible in about 5~7 minutes. 1. The teacher will tell you your question number. 2. Memorize your question. 3. Ask. 4. Make simple notes.

1. What age do you think is a good age to get married?	2. Do you know how your parents met?	3. How much money are you happy to spend for a Valentine's date?	4. Which is more important, a spouse who is really rich or really good looking and stylish?
5. Would you try omiai in order to find your partner?	6. Do you currently have a boy/girlfriend? How long have you been dating?	7. What is your favorite romantic movie?	8. Do you have a favorite celebrity you would like to date? Who?
9. Do you think it's ok to kiss on the first date?	10. Would you marry someone from a different country or culture?	11. Do you believe in love at first sight?	12. What's a good idea for a date that costs little money?
13. What's a good idea for a first date?	14. Have you ever given or received flowers from your boy/girlfriend?	15. Would you prefer a traditional Japanese-style or Western-style wedding?	16. Where would you like to go on your honeymoon?
17. How old were you when you had your first romantic kiss?	18. Have you ever had a broken heart?	19. Have you ever written a love letter?	20. What is a love song you really like?

LOVE ONE, LOVE ALL — LOVE SURVEY REPORTING

PART B: Report the results of your survey to your partner(s). First, report your classmates' answers. Then, tell your own answer. Follow this example:

I asked (total number of people), (question). (number of people) said ____________ (number of people) said ____________, and one person said ____________. My answer is ____________.

EXAMPLE: "I asked 9 people, 'What age do you think is a good age to get married?' Four people said 25, 3 people said 27, 1 person said 30, and 1 person said 35. My answer is ____________."

LOVE ONE, LOVE ALL — STEPS TO A LIFE OF LOVE

Falling in love can happen in an instant, but the process of meeting someone, falling in love, becoming a couple, and getting married usually has an order of occurrence. Put the following steps in the order you think they happen (1~12). Then, discuss with your partner(s) why you think so.

____ have children	____ go on honeymoon
____ get married	____ grow old together
____ first date	____ fall in love
____ meet someone you like	____ attraction/curiosity
____ really like	____ become a couple
____ get engaged	____ move in together

LOVE ONE, LOVE ALL — VOCABULARY & IDIOMS

Look at the love words and idioms in the box. Put an ○ next to the ones you know, and an × next to the ones you don't know. Compare with your partner(s). Then, explain some of the words you know but your partner(s) do not.

____ go steady	____ double date
____ love bite	____ arranged marriage
____ lovebirds	____ on the rocks
____ love is blind	____ widowed
____ lovesick	____ spouse
____ head over heels	____ blind date
____ a crush	____ bridegroom
____ affectionate	____ cheat
____ propose	____ pop the question

SMARTPHONE SMARTEN UP

You have 5 minutes to search for as many of the following answers as possible:

1. How is falling in love like being on drugs?
2. What is the effect on the body of hugging your partner?
3. What is an example of an animal that is monogamous?
4. What is the number one reason people get married?
5. What are some health benefits of being in love?
6. What is really important to keeping a relationship strong?
7. Does spending time away from your partner strengthen or weaken the relationship?
8. Who generally falls in love faster, men or women?

WHO SAID THAT? FAMOUS QUOTATIONS

Talk about these quotations with your partner(s). What do you think they mean?

"It is better to have loved and lost than never to have loved at all."
— Alfred Tennyson (poet, British, 1809-1892)

"Love isn't something you find. Love finds you."
— Loretta Young (actress, American, 1913-2000)

"Life is the flower for which love is the honey."
— Victor Hugo (writer/poet, French, 1802-1885)

Unit 12 Money and Finance, Dollars and Sense

PHOTO TALK Chat freely about the photo with your partner(s). What does it tell you about today's topic?

VOCABULARY Match the words and sentences (careful of word form).

In the spaces, write: the word in Japanese / a synonym in English

A.	poverty	/	F.	pay off	/
B.	currency	/	G.	impulse buying	/
C.	adopt	/	H.	expenditure	/
D.	associate with	/	I.	visualize	/
E.	debt	/	J.	self-esteem	/

1. The Japanese yen was ______________ in 1871.
2. America may be a very rich country, but many people still live in ______________.
3. Wendy borrowed some money from the bank, but she ______________ in 6 months.
4. It's important to ______________ positive people. They will make your life better.
5. ______________ can be fun, but it's also an easy way to waste money.
6. My art teacher said, "______________ the mountains and sky, then draw a picture."
7. Joan finally got a job. She saved some money, and she's no longer in ______________.
8. Most countries have their own ______________. Japan uses the yen; America, the dollar.
9. As her ______________ grows, Satoko knows she can achieve her goals!
10. Recently, my monthly ______________ are more than my income. Life is expensive!

Read All About It

Money and Finance, Dollars and Sense

13

1. Money. Everyone wants it. Everyone needs it. Some people have a lot of it; others will live their entire lives in **poverty**. Some say it is the **root** of all **evil**; others say it makes the world go around. Every country in the world uses money, but not every country has its own **currency**. Several countries use the US dollar (US$), and 19 countries in the Eurozone use the euro (€).

2. Money is the value of a currency. We buy things with money, and the currency represents its value. For example, 100 Japanese yen today buys less than it did 20 years ago, but the currency itself has not changed. The word money is from *moneta*, a Latin word for coin. The world's oldest currency still in use today is the British pound sterling (£ or GBP), dating back 1,200 years. The world's newest currency is the South Sudanese pound (SS£), introduced in 2011. The Japanese yen (¥ or JPY) was **adopted** by the Meiji government on June 27, 1871.

3. Finance involves activities **associated with** banking such as savings, credit, **debt**, and investments. Therefore, finance is about money **management**. Being good with money means to balance your **budget** properly, to avoid debt, and to grow **wealth**. While most people do work for the **reward** of being paid money, bankers, traders, and investors make money by working with money. Money alone does not lead to increased wealth. It's how you **manage** your money that **matters**. Some financial advice to consider includes these tips:

4. 1. Know your budget: spend within your limits. 2. Save: don't **waste** money. 3. **Avoid** credit cards: pay by a debit card or cash. 4. Read: learn about financing. 5. **Pay off** debt: if you owe money, pay it back as soon as possible. 6. Think: before making a major purchase (such as buying a car or home), research and compare. Avoid **impulse buying** of smaller items too (such as new clothes). 7. Cut back: reduce monthly **expenditures** such as phone and internet bills. 8. Do more with less: learn new ways to enjoy your life without spending money. 9. Pay attention: check your monthly bills to **visualize** your financial situation. 10. Ask for advice: speak to someone you know who is good with money. 11. Plan: think ahead 10, 20, 30+ years. You want to **retire** with **plenty** of money!

5. Most people will tell you that they would like to have a lot of money, to be really rich. But being super rich **demands** social responsibility to pay your share of taxes, to be **generous** by helping the less **fortunate**, and to support projects for the public good such as schools, hospitals, and the arts. No amount of money, however, can buy you happiness, love, purpose, time, family, friendships, manners, confidence, **self-esteem**, trust, inner peace, positivity, kindness, respect, truth, talent, or good **sense**.

Comprehension: Money and Finance

Answer the Questions. Write short answers.

1. What is the difference between money and currency?
2. What are 3 ways to avoid debt?
3. Why do most people desire to be rich?
4. Why is being super rich challenging?
5. What are some things that money cannot buy?

Complete the Sentences. Choose the best option or options.

6. The word “money” is from the French / Greek / Latin word “moneta”.
7. The Japanese yen was introduced in 1821 / 1851 / 1871.
8. Increasing wealth comes from saving salary / managing money / spending money.
9. Finance involves debt / shopping / credit.
10. There are 15 / 19 / 23 countries that use the Euro.

True (T) or False (F). If false, correct the sentence to make it true.

11. T / F: “Money is the root of all evil” means money can destroy people.
12. T / F: Having a lot of money will solve all problems.
13. T / F: “Money makes the world go around” means money makes things happen.
14. T / F: Using cash instead of credit cards can help avoid debt.
15. T / F: The value of a currency can change even if the currency itself does not change.

MONEY AND FINANCE, DOLLARS AND SENSE CURRENCIES

PART A: Match the **countries** with their **currency**, **letter code**, **currency symbol**.

10 Mongolia	Q / M13	1. Baht	A. EUR	A1. ₩
____ Canada	____ / ____	2. Renminbi	B. INR	B2. RM
____ Thailand	____ / ____	3. Birr	C. ZAR	C3. ₽
____ Israel	____ / ____	4. Krona	D. ARS	D4. E£
____ South Africa	____ / ____	5. Peso	E. SEK	E5. CN¥
____ Malaysia	____ / ____	6. Lira	F. ETB	F6. R
____ China	____ / ____	7. Shekel	G. CAD	G7. R$
____ South Korea	____ / ____	8. Won	H. USD	H8. $
____ France	____ / ____	9. Euro	I. MYR	I9. CA$
____ India	____ / ____	10. Tughrik	J. RUB	J10. Kr
____ Ethiopia	____ / ____	11. Rupee	K. CNY	K11. ₪
____ Brazil	____ / ____	12. Real	L. THB	L12. Br
____ Sweden	____ / ____	13. Rand	M. TRY	M13. ₮
____ Russia	____ / ____	14. Balboa	N. KRW	N14. US$
____ Argentina	____ / ____	15. Dollar	O. BRL	O15. €
____ Panama	____ / ____	16. US dollar	P. PAB	P16. ₹
____ Egypt	____ / ____	17. Rubl	Q. MNT	Q17. ₫
____ Vietnam	____ / ____	18. Dong	R. EGP	R18. ฿
____ Palau	____ / ____	19. Pound	S. ILS	S19. ₺
____ Turkey	____ / ____	20. Ringgit	T. VND	T20. B/

MONEY AND FINANCE, DOLLARS AND SENSE QUESTIONS

Talk about these money questions with your partner(s).

1. What does money do?
2. Do you remember the first time you earned some money? Describe it.
3. What is something you don't have enough money to do or buy?
4. What is the most expensive thing (or experience) you have ever bought?
5. How much money is a good monthly salary for 1 person?
6. Why is it important to save money? Are you saving now for something?
7. Do you know how much money your parents make? (Shhh, don't tell if you do!).
8. What is something you want to buy and need to buy?
9. Do you regret spending money on something?
10. What is debt? Is it good or bad?

MONEY AND FINANCE, DOLLARS AND SENSE COST OF LIVING

Life is expensive. Talk with your partner(s) about the costs of these things. Write down how much you think they cost. Answers may differ from your partner(s).

monthly rent for a 2LDK apartment (in Tokyo but outside the Yamanote line)	a new car	weekly food bill (1 person)	a roundtrip plane ticket Tokyo-New York
monthly electric bill for 2LDK apartment	a washing machine	monthly internet connection at home	university fees for 1 year
a light bulb	a double-size futon	jeans (average quality)	monthly water bill for 2LDK apartment

Think of a few other items or experiences and add them to the squares.

SMARTPHONE SMARTEN UP

You have 5 minutes to search for as many of the following answers as possible:

1. There are 7 US currency notes in circulation. What are they?
2. How much Japanese money is in circulation?
3. What is the total value of the 4 Japanese currency notes in circulation?
4. Can you still use a banknote if it is torn in half?
5. Where is Japanese money made?
6. What is the world's oldest currency still in use?
7. How much does it cost to make 1 US penny?
8. Which costs more to make, a US 10 cent or 5 cent coin?

WHO SAID THAT? FAMOUS QUOTATIONS

Talk about these quotations with your partner(s). What do you think they mean?

"A fool and his money are soon parted."
— Thomas Tusser (poet/farmer, English, 1524-1580)

"There's no such thing as a free lunch."
— Milton Friedman (economist, American, 1912-2006)

"I don't care too much for money, for money can't buy me love."
— The Beatles, "Can't Buy Me Love" (rock group, British, 1964)

Unit 13 Careers: Nice Job!

PHOTO TALK Chat freely about the photos with your partner(s). What do they tell you about today's topic?

VOCABULARY Match the words and sentences (careful of word form).

In the spaces, write: the word in Japanese / a synonym in English

A.	significant	/	F.	tackle	/
B.	suitable	/	G.	foster	/
C.	in the long run	/	H.	competitive	/
D.	income	/	I.	motivate	/
E.	accomplishment	/	J.	competent	/

1. Our holiday cost a ______________ amount of money, but we all had the best time!
2. Products and services are improved with a ______________ fight between businesses.
3. My wife received a very nice increase in ______________, but she's still underpaid!
4. The best way to solve a problem is to ______________ it before it becomes bigger.
5. Sending a man to the moon was a great ______________ in human history.
6. The boss is normally very ______________, but she made a big mistake this time.
7. It takes time to ______________ new friendships. Making friends takes effort.
8. I know you're not very happy these days, but I have an idea to ______________ you.
9. You can't wear a t-shirt to a wedding! You have to wear ______________ clothing!
10. You studied hard, and ______________, you succeeded and got a great job!

Read All About It

Careers: Nice Job!

14

1. A career is an occupation, a job, that someone does for a **significant** part of one's adult work life. As a university student, you are probably thinking a lot about what work you would like to do after you graduate. You may already be job hunting or working part-time. Choosing a career is difficult for most people. With so many options and personal interests, finding a **suitable** job is a job in itself.

2. But what does it mean to have a "good" job? A big salary? A happy work environment? Opportunities to travel? Meeting different kinds of people? Job security? Most people would answer: "Money!" While money is important in many ways, **in the long run**, job **fulfillment** outweighs **income**.

3. Having a career or even part-time employment has many benefits in addition to **earning** money. Employment brings social connections and opportunities to learn. Contributing positively to a business gives you a sense of pride and **accomplishment**. Seeing results of your hard work is pleasing. Work gives us purpose, goals, and personal worth. Employment **encourages** us to think and to **tackle** challenges. A job makes us visible to other people, as well as **recognized** and valued by others. Working with other people **fosters** social and community harmony. Some careers provide opportunities and benefits such as healthcare, paid holidays, education, skills training, and friendships.

4. It's a **competitive** world, and getting a job can be harder than actually doing the job. There are many **strategies**, however, for finding the right career for you. Strategies will help **motivate** you, focus your efforts, and save you time and stress. The first strategy is to think of job hunting as a job in itself. Other strategies may include:

5. *Identify your goals:* consider not only what type of work you want to do, but in what way. Most careers involve various types of work associated with that career. Identifying goals means recognizing your skill set, your personality type, what motivates you, and understanding your strengths and weaknesses. *Think ahead:* consider long-term goals and plans, including those in your personal life. Be **tech-savvy**: keep your technical skills up-to-date. *Develop leadership and communication skills:* these **abilities** show you are confident and **competent**. *Network:* talk to people, go to job fairs, join a professional group. *Keep your eyes open:* starting a new career usually means starting at the bottom and working your way up, so look for jobs in unexpected places. *Be resilient:* don't let job **rejection** get you down. Be positive, and knock on more doors. *Build a strong CV* (curriculum vitae, or résumé). Your CV is the first impression an employer is likely to have of you. Make it look and read **professionally**.

6. Work is important, but so is fun. All work and no play makes Jack a **dull** boy.

Comprehension: Nice Job!

Answer the Questions. Write short answers.

1. What is a career?
2. What makes choosing a career so difficult for many people?
3. Besides money, what sorts of advantages does having a career give people?
4. What are some strategies to finding a job?
5. What does the last line mean, "All work and no play makes Jack a dull boy"?

Complete the Sentences. Choose the best option or options.

6. Good communication skills show a person is confident / smart / likes to talk.
7. A good job means a big salary / security / happiness.
8. Networking means to work different jobs / meeting people / working on the internet.
9. A CV is often / sometimes / always the first impression an employer has of you.
10. Most / A few / Some people find job hunting harder than doing the job itself.

True (T) or False (F). If false, correct the sentence to make it true.

11. T / F: It's easier to find a job than to do a job.
12. T / F: Being tech-savvy means to be up-to-date on how to use technology.
13. T / F: A career is one specific job over a long period of time.
14. T / F: There are only a few key strategies for job and career hunting.
15. T / F: Over time, being fulfilled with work is more important than earning a big salary.

CAREERS: NICE JOB! DESCRIBING JOBS

Work with your partner(s) to match and write job descriptions. There are more jobs listed in the box than there are in the descriptions, however.

dentist / painter / architect / baker / butcher / electrician / engineer
firefighter / florist / hairdresser / journalist / lawyer / optician / tailor
pharmacist / plumber / carpenter / politician / scientist / mechanic
veterinarian / police officer / travel agent / waiter-waitress / accountant

_______________ : keeps and inspects financial records and taxes

architect : ____

_______________ : makes bread and cakes and normally works in a bakery

butcher : ____

carpenter : ____

_______________ : can fix problems you have with your teeth

electrician : ____

_______________ : designs, builds, or maintains engines, machines, structures or public works

_______________ : puts out fires and oversees safety of public buildings

florist : ____

hairdresser : ____

_______________ : reports the news on television and in other media

lawyer : ____

mechanic : ____

_______________ : checks the eyes and corrects vision problems

painter : ____

_______________ : works with and dispenses medicines (drugs)

veterinarian : ____

waiter/waitress : ____

CAREERS: NICE JOB! DESCRIBING JOBS

With your partner(s), consider all of the jobs on the list. Which do you think you could you possibly do, and which would be impossible for you to do? Explain.

A. Which of these jobs do you think is the highest paying?
B. Which of these jobs do you think are the easiest and hardest to do? Why?
C. Which of these jobs do you think needs the most training and education? Why?
D. Which of these jobs do you think are the most and least fun? Why?
E. Which of these jobs do you think is the most important? Why?

WOULD YOU RATHER ... ?

PART A: Choosing a suitable job requires considering many aspects, features, tasks, and responsibilities of the work. Take turns asking and answering the following "would you rather" questions with your partner(s).

Would you rather ... ?

A. ... work inside ____ or outside ____

B. ... wear a uniform ____, formal clothes ____, or casual clothes ____

C. ... work with a team ____ or by yourself ____

D. ... work for yourself ____ or for an employer ____

E. ... go to an office ____, work from home ____, or travel around ____

F. ... work business hours (Mon-Fri, 9AM-5:30PM) ____ or irregular hours ____

G. ... do an easy job ____ or a challenging job ____

H. ... work full-time ____ or part-time ____

I. ... get a big salary but stressed ____ or an ok salary but relaxed ____

J. ... have a lot of responsibility ____ or little or no responsibility ____

K. ... Ask your own "would you rather" question.

ADDITIONAL COMMENTS. After asking and answering the questions, go back to get some extra information about some of them. Make notes here:

PART B: Consider the answers and information your classmate told you. Suggest a job or two that they could possibly do. Respond to each other's suggestions. For example, tell your classmate: "Based on your comments, I think you should be a ______________ or possibly a ______________ because ____(explain)____."

PART C: Look back at the Photo Talk photos. With your partner(s), discuss the pros and cons of each of the 4 jobs. What sorts of responsibilities and challenges does each one have?

CAREERS: NICE JOB! THE CAREER PLANNING CHECKLIST

Work with your partner(s). Read the checklist items and choose your answers. Of course, each classmate's answers will be different. This checklist will help you to determine if you are ready for job hunting or what you need to do to prepare. Choose: Y = yes / N = no / P = partly.

My Career Planning checklist

	WHAT I KNOW ABOUT MY PRIMARY CAREER INTEREST
Y / N / P 1.	I know the work duties and responsibilities that match my interests.
Y / N / P 2.	I know what sorts of work experiences are important for my career.
Y / N / P 3.	I know several skills I can use for my career.
Y / N / P 4.	I know what skills I need to obtain and/or improve.
	CAREER CHOICES AND ALTERNATIVES
Y / N / P 5.	I know different job titles that match my areas of work interest.
Y / N / P 6.	I know what education and background is required for my career.
Y / N / P 7.	I know several businesses or companies that suit my job interests.
Y / N / P 8.	I have talked to people who already do this kind of job.
	ACQUIRING EXPERIENCE
Y / N / P 9.	I have decided my major area of study at university.
Y / N / P 10.	I am taking classes that are related to the job I want.
Y / N / P 11.	I participate in activities or a part-time job related to my career.
Y / N / P 12.	I am doing an internship or volunteering to get experience.
	JOB HUNTING
Y / N / P 13.	I can clearly and simply communicate my career interests and goals.
Y / N / P 14.	I know what kinds of companies will hire someone like me.
Y / N / P 15.	I know how to write a cover letter and a strong CV (résumé).
Y / N / P 16.	I have researched several of the companies I am interested in.
	JOB INTERVIEWING
Y / N / P 17.	I understand how the interview process works.
Y / N / P 18.	I have practiced my interview skills with friends or professionals.
Y / N / P 19.	I know how to improve my interview skills.
Y / N / P 20.	I am confident when I go to interviews.

SMARTPHONE SMARTEN UP

You have 5 minutes to search for as many of the following answers as possible:

1. What day of the week is the most common sick day?
2. What day of the week is the least common sick day?
3. Who wrote the first CV (résumé)?
4. What does the word “boss” mean in Dutch?
5. How many hours a week do people work in France?
6. How many employees does McDonald’s in Japan have?
7. What is the average annual (yearly) salary in Japan for a full-time worker?
8. Do your school and university grades matter to an employer?

WHO SAID THAT? FAMOUS QUOTATIONS

Talk about these quotations with your partner(s). What do you think they mean?

“Find a job you enjoy doing, and you will never have to work a day in your life..”
— Mark Twain (writer, American, 1983-1910)

“Laziness may appear attractive, but work gives satisfaction.”
— Anne Frank (diarist, German, 1929-1945)

“The harder I work, the luckier I get.”
— Samuel Goldwyn (film producer, Polish-American, 1879-1974)

Unit 14 Across the Universe: If Earth Were a Cherry Tomato

PHOTO TALK Chat freely about the photo with your partner(s). What does it tell you about today's topic?

VOCABULARY Match the words and sentences (careful of word form).

In the spaces, write: the word in Japanese / a synonym in English

A.	mind-boggling	/	F.	solar system	/
B.	immense	/	G.	astonishing	/
C.	observable	/	H.	dimension	/
D.	vastness	/	I.	squeeze	/
E.	rotate	/	J.	mammal	/

1. Their new house is ________________. It has 7 bedrooms, 5 bathrooms, and 4 floors!
2. The ________________ of space is impossible to really understand. Earth is a tiny thing.
3. Whales are large ________________ that live in the sea.
4. His measurements of the ________________ of the room were not very accurate.
5. The Earth ________________ once every 24 hours. This is called a day.
6. The ship was ________________ from the beach until it reached the horizon.
7. I had a very busy day, but I ________________ in time for lunch with my best friend.
8. It's ________________ how many people believe in fake news. It's truly unbelievable.
9. Neptune is the furthest planet in our ________________. It is 4,472,800,000 kilometers from Earth.
10. It's ________________ that scientists are still discovering new animals and types of fish.

Read All About It

15

Across the Universe: If Earth Were a Cherry Tomato

1. The scale of the universe is mind-boggling. It is so **immense** that astronomers (people who study space) believe only 4% of the known universe is **observable**. The entire universe is at least 250 times larger than what we can see. But what does that really mean? The **vastness** of the universe is one of the most challenging things for humans to comprehend.

2. Earth is about 384,000 kilometers (km) from the Moon and about 150,000,000 km from the Sun. Traveling by car non-stop at 100 km/h (hour), it would take about 160 days to reach the moon and 170 years to the Sun! Distances in space are so vast that they are measured in **light years** — how far light travels in a year. Light travels at 300,000 km/s (second), or about 7.5 times around the Earth. **Thus**, in one year, light travels 9,700,000,000,000 kilometers.

3. Another way of **visualizing** distances in space is to think of the planets as a number of steps from the Sun: Mercury is 1 step from the Sun, Venus is 2 steps, Earth is 2.5 steps, Mars is 4 steps, Jupiter is 13 steps, Saturn is 24 steps, Uranus, is 49 steps, and Neptune is 76 steps.

4. Each day, about half a million people are born and die on Earth, and about 275 million stars begin or end. Earth travels around the Sun once a year, but it takes the Sun 225 million years to **rotate** around the Milky Way, the **galaxy** that includes our **solar system**. It's about 100,000 light years across and filled with 100-400,000,000 stars and even more planets. When you look at the night sky, you can see about 2,500 stars, but there are at least 224,000,000,000. Earth travels about 107,000 km/h, or about 2.6 million km a day. In a year, humans travel about 149,597,870 kilometers around the Sun.

5. Equally **astonishing** to these incredible distances is the relative size of the planets and stars. Earth's **circumference** at the equator is about 40,000 km. About 50 Moons could fit inside the Earth, but more than 1,000,000 Earth's can fit inside the Sun. The biggest star in the universe is UY Scuti which can hold 3,690,000,000 Suns. If Earth is a cherry tomato, Mercury is a peppercorn, Venus is a grape, Mars is a blueberry, Jupiter is a watermelon, Saturn is a grapefruit, Uranus is an apple, and Neptune is an orange.

6. Time itself is a **dimension** of space. It takes light about 8.3 minutes to travel from the Sun to Earth, but 5.2 billion years from UY Scuti to Earth. If all of time is **squeezed** into one human year, each day represents 38 million years. And if the Big Bang, the start of the universe, is January 1, then Earth was **formed** in mid-September, **mammals** appeared on December 26, and all of human history has happened a few minutes before **midnight** on December 31.

Comprehension: Across the Universe

Answer the Questions. Write short answers.

1. What does "the scale of the universe is mind-boggling" mean?
2. Why are distances in space measured in light years?
3. Why do people use different ways of visualizing the sizes and distances of planets?
4. Why is time a dimension?
5. If all of time were squeezed into one calendar year, when does human activity begin?

Complete the Sentences. Choose the best option or options.

6. Earth is about 280,000 / 380,000 / 480,000 kilometers from the Moon.
7. The Sun can hold about 100,000 / 1,000,000 / 1,000,000,000 Earths.
8. It takes light about 10,000 / 100,000 / 1,000,000 years to travel across the Milky Way.
9. Earth is the closest / second closest / third closet planet to the Sun.
10. Each day, about 275,000,000 / 375,000,000 / 475,000,000 stars are born.

True (T) or False (F). If false, correct the sentence to make it true.

11. T / F: It takes about 8.3 minutes for light from the Sun to reach Earth.
12. T / F: Driving to the Moon at 100 km/h would take about a month.
13. T / F: The Sun stays in one place in the galaxy.
14. T / F: Looking at the night sky, we can see about 2,500 stars.
15. T / F: The Sun is the biggest star in our solar system.

ACROSS THE UNIVERSE THE PLANETS

How much do you know about the planets? Work with your partner(s) to complete the following information.

8 planets orbit the Sun. In the spaces to the right of the letters, unscramble and write the planet names. Next, in the smaller spaces on the left, write the order of the planets from the Sun. Finally, in the parentheses (____), write the letter of their distances from the Sun. You must choose from the two distances listed for each.

<u>4</u> rsam : <u>Mars</u> (<u>D1</u>)		____ teupnen : ____________ (____)
____ rnstau : ____________ (____)		____ svnue : ____________ (____)
____ htera : ____________ (____)		____ sanuru : ____________ (____)
____ remcuyr : ____________ (____)		____ iptjeur : ____________ (____)

A1: 37.54 / A2: 57.91 million km	E1: 698.9 / E2: 778.5 million km
B1: 92.3 / B2: 108.2 million km	F1: 1.12 / F2: 1.434 billion km
C1: 149.6 / C2: 172.22 million km	G1: 1.97 / G2: 2.871 billion km
D1: 227.9 / D2: 332.2 million km	H1: 4.495 / H2: 4.722 billion km

ACROSS THE UNIVERSE PLANET FACTS

T = True or F= False. Work with your partner(s) to answer the questions.

T / F 1. The surface temperature of Venus is about -460 degrees Celsius.
T / F 2. The largest volcano in the solar system is on Earth.
T / F 3. Saturn's rings are made of water droplets.
T / F 4. Earth is larger than Mercury, Venus, and Neptune.
T / F 5. Uranus is a gas planet.
T / F 6. Mars is between Earth and Venus.
T / F 7. Neptune is the coldest planet.
T / F 8. Saturn has 62 moons.
T / F 9. Mars is known as the "Red Planet".
T / F 10. Jupiter is the stormiest planet.

ACROSS THE UNIVERSE | BE A STAR — 12 QUESTIONS

Talk freely with your partner(s) about the following question.

1. What fascinates you about the universe?	2. Do you think space is infinite?	3. If you could go to any planet, which would you choose and why?	4. Is there life somewhere else in the universe?
5. Would you rather travel to the moon or to the bottom of the deepest part of the ocean?	6. Would you like to meet an alien?	7. Do you think humans understand a lot or a little about the universe?	8. Do you think humans will ever inhabit another planet?
9. Do you like space movies?	10. Is space travel worth the cost?	11. Do you like astronomy?	12. Do you believe in astrology?

Do you have more questions? Go ahead. Be a star — ask them!

SMARTPHONE SMARTEN UP

You have 5 minutes to search for as many of the following answers as possible:

1. What is astronomy?
2. What is a shooting star?
3. Which is greater, the number of stars in the universe or the number of grains of sand on all the world's beaches?
4. How old is Earth?
5. What effect does the Moon have on Earth?
6. How long is one day on Mercury (in Earth days)?
7. What direction do most planets travel around the sun?
8. Why are the footprints on the Moon still there?

WHO SAID THAT? FAMOUS QUOTATIONS

Talk about these quotations with your partner(s). What do you think they mean?

"The universe is under no obligation to make sense to you."
— Neil deGrasse Tyson (astrophysicist, American, 1958-)

"We are an impossibility in an impossible universe."
— Ray Bradbury (writer, American, 1920-2012)

"The universe is a pretty big place. If it's just us, seems like an awful waste of space."
— Carl Sagan (astronomer, American, 1934-1996)

Unit 15 Risks: Take Your Chances

PHOTO TALK Chat freely about the image with your partner(s). What does it tell you about today's topic?

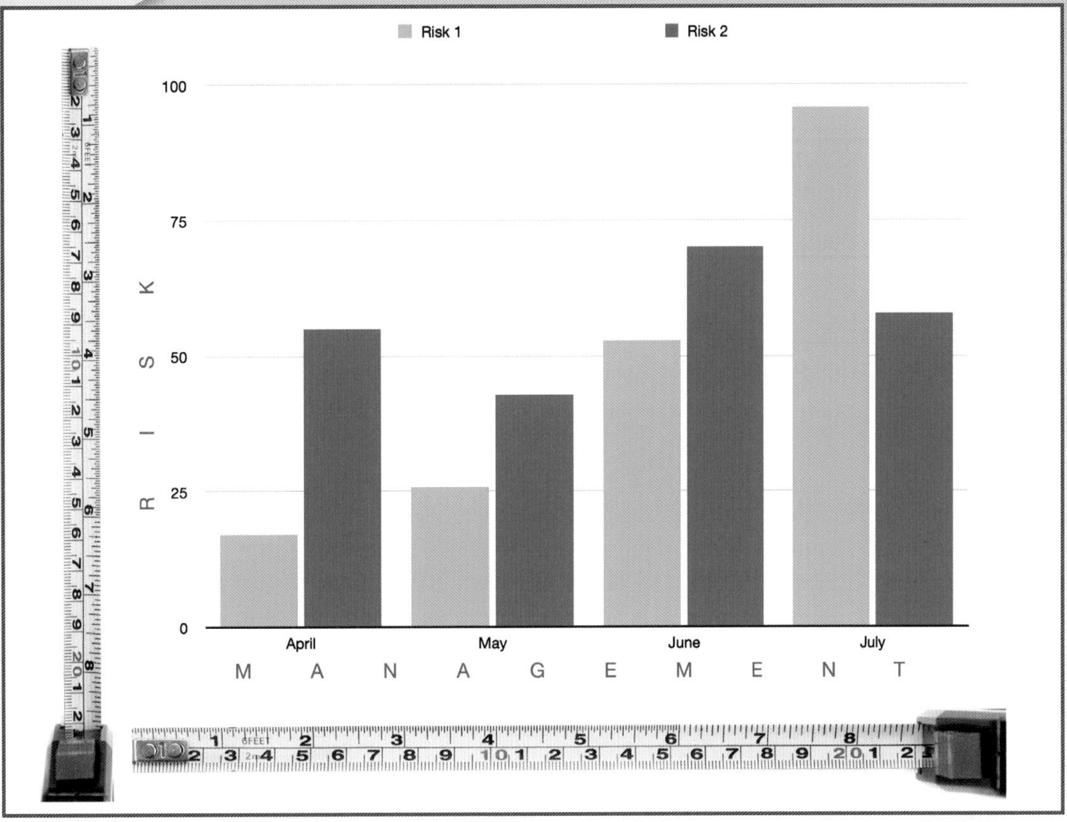

VOCABULARY Match the words and sentences (careful of word form).

In the spaces, write: the word in Japanese / a synonym in English

A.	cautious	/	F.	vitality	/
B.	inherent	/	G.	attain	/
C.	degree	/	H.	essential	/
D.	residual	/	I.	stimulate	/
E.	boost	/	J.	comfort zone	/

1. She's a ________________ driver, but she still crashed the car.
2. ________________ radiation around Fukushima nuclear plant will remain for many years.
3. It is ________________ to eat fresh, balanced foods to keep good health.
4. Riding a motorcycle is ________________ dangerous. Someday, you will have an accident.
5. The dogs were running in the park with great ________________. It was so fun to watch them.
6. Paying the workers more money ________________ production. Business is booming!
7. She took a trip by herself to get out of her ________________ and experience new things.
8. There is a ________________ of truth in what he said, but mostly he's incorrect.
9. Learning to speak English ________________ opportunities to meet new people.
10. I will not ________________ peace of mind until I find my missing dog. I'm so upset.

Risks: Take Your Chances

16

1. "Opportunity does not come gift-wrapped. You must take risks." This expression means you cannot wait for things to happen in life, you have to take chances to make them happen. Taking a risk means to take a chance on something. Risk by definition **involves** the possibility of loss, disappointment, or even danger.

2. Not all risks are equal. A **calculated risk** is a chance taken after considering the **degree** of a negative outcome. Some people take **huge** risks with their money or their lives. Most people, however, are more **cautious**. But life is **inherently** full of risks: investing money, crossing the street, or riding in a car all have some **degree** of risk. We cannot control every **aspect** of life. Even after taking as many **precautions** as possible, some risk remains. This is called **residual risk**.

3. Men are generally bigger risk-takers than women. But taking reasonable risks is important for everyone. Doing so **boosts** confidence and **reduces** the fear of failing. Risks add **vitality** and excitement to life, for example, traveling on your own. By taking risks, unexpected things can happen such as a new experience, meeting new people, or finding a job opportunity. Risks that fail teach us how to do things differently or better. Risks lead to success. Taking risks helps dreams come true.

4. Think of any really successful person — Tadashi Yanai, Albert Einstein, Yayoi Kusama, Bill Gates, Walt Disney. All of them took huge risks in order to **attain** their goals and dreams. Few people will be as well-known or as wealthy, but everyone has to take risks to find their own success. "Playing it safe" — to be **overly** cautious — leads to **regrets**. It is better to take risks and fail than never to have tried. Risk-taking, therefore, is an **essential** part of life. It helps us find meaning and shapes our lives. We only have one life, but we can have as many chances as we create for ourselves.

5. Life's greatest moments and **achievements** come from taking risks. It may be overcoming shyness by making a speech in front of many people, investing money in a business, or taking a chance on love. By taking risks, people notice you. Risk creates change and **stimulates** you to do more. Risk teaches you things about yourself that you did not know before, for example, an untapped **ability** or a **limitation**.

6. Life without risk is boring. Imagine sitting at home all day, never going anywhere, not meeting new people, or rarely having a new adventure. Taking a risk does not mean risking your life. So what if you **embarrass** yourself? Get up and get out of your **comfort zone**, and step into the big world.

7. Life is a game of risk. Take your chances. No regrets.

Comprehension: Risks: Take Your Chances

Answer the Questions. Write short answers.

1. What does "opportunity does not come gift-wrapped" mean?
2. What is a risk? Explain what it means.
3. What is a calculated risk?
4. What is residual risk?
5. What are some advantages of taking risks?

Complete the Sentences. Choose the best option or options.

6. Being too cautious leads to greater security / regrets / an increase in confidence.
7. Playing it safe means to take small risks / be overly cautious / avoid embarrassment.
8. Taking risks is important for only some people / famous people / everyone.
9. Risk involves the chance / certainty / doubt of loss, disappointment, or danger.
10. Risk creates change / danger / failure.

True (T) or False (F). If false, correct the sentence to make it true.

11. T / F: Women are bigger risk takers than men.
12. T / F: The most successful people all take risks.
13. T / F: Taking risks helps us find meaning in our lives.
14. T / F: Risks sometimes fail, but not trying can be more regrettable than never trying.
15. T / F: Life without risk is boring because nothing happens.

RISKS: TAKE YOUR CHANCES | LIFE IS FULL OF RISKS

What does it mean to take a risk?

PART A: What are some of the risks associated with the things in the risk box? Which ones have you taken? Add other risks to the box that you have personally taken. Next, consider these risks, and rank them 0 (low risk) to 10 (high risk).

- smoking
- texting while driving
- gambling
- eating too much sugar
- riding a bicycle
- drinking alcohol
- eating junk food
- driving a car
- poor dental hygiene
- failing
- Using the internet
- sunbathing

PART B: Talk freely with your partner(s) about these questions. You do not have to agree with one another, of course, but explain your thoughts, opinions, and ideas.

1. What is the biggest risk you have ever taken? What was the outcome?
2. What is a risk you think you could never take?
3. Have you ever regretted taking a risk? Explain.
4. Have you ever wished you took a bigger risk on something you did?
5. What do you think is the biggest daily risk you face each day? Is is avoidable?
6. Do you always follow safety rules such as wearing a seat belt?
7. Is there a place you don't usually feel safe?
8. Would you ever pick up a hitchhiker? Why or why not?
9. Would you risk your life to save someone?
10. Do you think travel involves more risks than daily life at home? Explain.
11. Who is a famous risk-taker you admire? Why?
12. Why do some people take big risks and other people do not?

RISKS: TAKE YOUR CHANCES | CALCULATING YOUR RISK LEVEL

Consider these statements to calculate how big of a risk-taker you are. Discuss them with your partner(s), but enter only your own scores.

1 low > 5 high risk

1.	I consider myself to be a risk-taker.	1	2	3	4	5
2.	I am not afraid to try and fail at something.	1	2	3	4	5
3.	I like trying new things.	1	2	3	4	5
4.	I like challenges.	1	2	3	4	5
5.	I like feeling scared sometimes.	1	2	3	4	5
6.	I don't always want to follow the rules.	1	2	3	4	5
7.	I like talking to strangers.	1	2	3	4	5
8.	I like to do physical activities such as hiking and skiing.	1	2	3	4	5
9.	I do things that my parents would disapprove of.	1	2	3	4	5
10.	I prefer to spend money than to save money.	1	2	3	4	5
11.	I like to do things without thinking about the consequences.	1	2	3	4	5
12.	I think doing something is better than doing nothing.	1	2	3	4	5
13.	I feel excited when I do something risky.	1	2	3	4	5
14.	I admire people who take risks.	1	2	3	4	5
15.	I need to take more risks in my life.	1	2	3	4	5

POINTS: /75

YOUR SCORE:

15~25: You are a low risk taker.
26~35: You are a low risk taker, but you are curious about taking more risks.
36~45: You are moderate risk taker.
46~55: You are a risk taker but you are cautious.
56~65: You are a risk taker.
66~75: You are a high risk taker!

How does your score compare to other classmates?
Talk to 2 more people and compare.

SMARTPHONE SMARTEN UP

You have 5 minutes to search for as many of the following answers as possible:

1. What is the world's riskiest job?
2. What are some of the riskiest sports?
3. What is the world's most deadly animal?
4. What is the riskiest type of transport?
5. What is the riskiest food people commonly eat?
6. What is the world's most infectious disease?
7. What is the most dangerous dog?
8. What is the riskiest food to eat in Japan?

WHO SAID THAT? FAMOUS QUOTATIONS

Talk about these quotations with your partner(s). What do you think they mean?

"He who is not courageous enough to take risks will accomplish nothing in life."
— Muhammed Ali (professional boxer, American, 1942-2016)

"You cannot swim for new horizons until you have courage to lose sight of the shore."
— William Faulkner (writer, American, 1897-1962)

"Be brave. Take risks. Nothing can substitute experience."
— Paulo Coelho (lyricist/novelist, Brazilian, 1947-)

NUMBERS

Numbers are important.

CARDINAL NUMBERS (1, 2, 3, etc) are used for counting amounts or to show "how many" of something, for example, "There are 20 students in the room."

ORDINAL NUMBERS (1st, 2nd, 3rd, etc.) are used to show order, rank, or position, for example, "I am the 1st person in line."

Use the chart below to review counting cardinal numbers.

It's easy, but remember these rules:

A. Numbers in English are counted by groups of three spaces.
B. Each group has a name, e.g. thousands.
C. So the number "123" = one hundred twenty three. But "123,456" = one hundred twenty three *thousand* four hundred fifty six. "123" is in the thousands group, so say "123+group name" then "456".
D. Just remember: numbers/group name, numbers/group name, numbers/group name.
E. But for numbers in the hundreds-tens-ones group, do *not* say a group name.

Forms of the Number Group Names: with and without "-s"

NOTE: The chart shows group names with -s because they are non-specific numbers.

Without "-s": For example, THOUSAND > Use for **specific numbers**, as follows ...

There are 12,345 students at this university.
There are twelve thousand, three hundred forty-five students at this university.
NOTE: Do not say "twelve thousand**s** ..."

With "-s": For example, MILLION**S** > Use for **non-specific numbers**, as follows ...

There are millions of people living in Tokyo.
Millions of people live in Tokyo.

Quadrillions			Trillions			Billions			Millions			Thousands					
Hundred Quadrillions	Ten Quadrillions	Quadrillions	Hundred Trillions	Ten Trillions	Trillions	Hundred Billions	Ten Billions	Billions	Hundred Millions	Ten Millions	Millions	Hundred Thousands	Ten Thousands	Thousands	Hundreds	Tens	Ones
8	7	6	5	4	3	2	1	5	2	1	7	3	6	4	9	5	8

GRAMMAR

English Tenses

	PRESENT	PAST	FUTURE
SIMPLE	1. The dog eats (on the bed every day).	2. The dog ate (on the bed).	3. The dog will eat (on the bed tonight).
CONTINUOUS (progressive)	4. The dog is eating (on the bed).	5. The dog was eating (on the bed).	6. The dog will be eating (on the bed tonight).
PERFECT	7. The dog has never eaten so much (on the bed).	8. The dog had eaten (on the bed by the time his owner came home).	9. The dog will have eaten all of his food (by this same time again tomorrow).
PERFECT CONTINUOUS (progressive)	10. The dog has been eating (on the bed for an hour).	11. The dog had been eating (on the bed for an hour when his owner came).	12. The dog will have been eating (on the bed when his owner comes home).

1. The dog eats on the bed everyday. It is his habit.
2. The dog ate on the bed. He finished eating. He is not eating now.
3. The dog plans to eat on the bed again. He is not eating now.
4. The dog is eating on the bed at this moment.
5. The dog was eating on the bed but not now — possibly while something else was happening at the same time. E.g. He was eating when his owner came home.
6. The dog has a future plan to eat on the bed — possibly while something else is happening. E.g. He will be eating on the bed while his owner watches TV.
7. The dog ate too much, and he had not eaten that much at any time before.
8. The dog had completed eating before his owner came home. He is not eating now.
9. The dog has some food. He will eat all of it by this time tomorrow. He will then have no more food.
10. The dog started eating 1 hour ago. He is still eating now. He is on the bed.
11. The dog started eating 1 hour before his owner came home. He probably continued eating after his owner got home, but he may have stopped.
12. The dog will start eating before his owner comes home, but he is not eating yet. The dog will probably continue eating after his owner comes home, or he may stop.

PRESENT SIMPLE

STRUCTURE

Positive: Subject + Main Verb (+ Object).

I drink coffee.

Negative: Subject + Auxiliary Verb + Not [do + not (don't)/does + not (doesn't)] + Main Verb (+ Object).

She doesn't drink coffee.

Question: Do/Does + Subject + Main Verb (+ Object)?

Positive: Do they drink coffee?

Negative: Do they not drink coffee? / Don't they drink coffee?

PAST SIMPLE

STRUCTURE

Positive: Subject + Main Verb [Past] (+ Object).

I drank coffee.

Negative: Subject + Auxiliary Verb + Not [did + not/didn't] + Main Verb (+ Object).

She didn't drink coffee.

Question: Auxiliary Verb [Did] + Subject + Main Verb [Past] (+ Object)?

Positive: Did they drink coffee?

Negative: Did they not drink coffee? / Didn't they drink coffee?

FUTURE SIMPLE

STRUCTURE

Positive: Subject + Auxiliary [will] + Main Verb (+ Object).

I will drink coffee.

Negative: Subject + Auxiliary + Not [will not/won't] + Main Verb (+ Object).

I will not drink coffee.

Question: Auxiliary Verb [Will] + Subject + Main Verb (+ Object)?

Positive: Will they drink coffee?

Negative: Will they not drink coffee? / Won't they drink coffee?

PRESENT CONTINUOUS

STRUCTURE

Positive: Subject + Auxiliary [be] + Main Verb -ing (+ Object).

I am drinking coffee.

Negative: Subject + Auxiliary [be] + Not [is not/isn't/are not/aren't} + Main Verb -ing (+ Object).

She is not drinking coffee.

Question: Auxiliary Verb [Will] + Subject + Auxiliary [be] + Main Verb -ing (+ Object)?

Positive: Are they drinking coffee?

Negative: Are they not drinking coffee? / Aren't they drinking coffee?

PAST CONTINUOUS

STRUCTURE

Positive: Subject + Auxiliary [was/were] + Main Verb -ing (+ Object).

I was drinking coffee.

Negative: Subject + Auxiliary + Not [was not/wasn't/were not/weren't] + Main Verb -ing (+ Object).

She was not drinking coffee.

Question: Auxiliary Verb [was/were] + Subject + Main Verb -ing (+ Object)?

Positive: Were they drinking coffee?

Negative: Were they not drinking coffee? / Weren't they drinking coffee?

FUTURE CONTINUOUS

STRUCTURE

Positive: Subject + Auxiliary [will] + be + Main Verb -ing (+ Object).

I will be drinking coffee.

Negative: Subject + Auxiliary + Not [will not/won't] + Auxiliary [be] + Main Verb -ing (+ Object).

She will not be drinking coffee.

Question: Auxiliary Verb [Will] + Subject + Auxiliary [be] + Main Verb -ing (+ Object)?

Positive: Will they be drinking coffee?

Negative: Will they not be drinking coffee? / Won't they be drinking coffee?

PRESENT PERFECT

STRUCTURE

Positive: Subject + Auxiliary [have/has] + Past Participle Verb (+ Object).

I have drunk coffee.

Negative: Subject + Auxiliary + Not [have not/haven't/has not/hasn't] + Past Participle Verb (+ Object).

She has not drunk coffee.

Question: Auxiliary Verb [have/has] + Subject + Past Participle Verb (+ Object)?

Positive: Have they drunk coffee?

Negative: Have they not drunk coffee? / Haven't they drunk coffee?

PAST PERFECT

STRUCTURE

Positive: Subject + Auxiliary [had] + Past Participle Verb (+ Object).

I had drunk coffee.

Negative: Subject + Auxiliary + Not [had not/hadn't] + Past Participle Verb (+ Object).

She had not drunk coffee.

Question: Auxiliary Verb [had] + Subject + Past Participle Verb (+ Object)?

Positive: Had they drunk coffee?

Negative: Had they not drunk coffee? / Hadn't they drunk coffee?

FUTURE PERFECT

STRUCTURE

Positive: Subject + Auxiliary [will] + Auxiliary [have] + Past Participle Verb (+ Object).

I will have drunk coffee.

Negative: Subject + Auxiliary + Not [will not/won't] + Auxiliary [have] + Past Participle Verb (+ Object).

She will not have drunk coffee.

Question: Auxiliary Verb [will] + Subject + Auxiliary [have] + Past Participle Verb (+ Object)?

Positive: Will they have drunk coffee?

Negative: Will they not have drunk coffee? / Won't they have drunk coffee?

PRESENT PERFECT CONTINUOUS

STRUCTURE

Positive: Subject + Auxiliary [have/has] + Auxiliary [been] + Main Verb -ing (+ Object).

I have been drinking coffee.

Negative: Subject + Auxiliary + Not [have not/haven't/has not/hasn't] + Auxiliary [been] + Main Verb -ing (+ Object).

She has not been drinking coffee.

Question: Auxiliary Verb [have/has] + Subject + Auxiliary [been] + Main Verb -ing (+ Object)?

Positive: Have they been drinking coffee?

Negative: Have they not been drinking coffee? / Haven't they been drinking coffee?

PAST PERFECT CONTINUOUS

STRUCTURE

Positive: Subject + Auxiliary [had] + Auxiliary [been] + Main Verb -ing (+ Object).

I had been drinking coffee.

Negative: Subject + Auxiliary + Not [had not/hadn't] + Auxiliary [been] + Main Verb -ing (+ Object).

She had not been drinking coffee.

Question: Auxiliary Verb [had] + Subject + Auxiliary [been] + Main Verb -ing (+ Object)?

Positive: Had they been drinking coffee?

Negative: Had they not been drinking coffee? / Hadn't they been drinking coffee?

FUTURE PERFECT CONTINUOUS

STRUCTURE

Positive: Subject + Auxiliary [will] + Auxiliary [have] + Auxiliary [been] + Main Verb -ing (+ Object).

I will have been drinking coffee.

Negative: Subject + Auxiliary + Not [will not/won't] + Auxiliary [have] + Auxiliary [been] + Main Verb -ing (+ Object).

She will not have been drinking coffee.

Question: Auxiliary Verb [will] + Subject + Auxiliary [have] + Auxiliary [been] + Main Verb -ing (+ Object)?

Positive: Will they have been drinking coffee?

Negative: Will they not have been drinking coffee? / Won't they have been drinking coffee?

PRESENT SIMPLE

PRESENT:
ALWAYS TRUE: People eat food.
PERMANENT SITUATIONS: Mt. Fuji is Japan's tallest mountain.
SHORT ACTIONS HAPPENING NOW: Smith shoots the ball and scores a goal!
HABITS and REGULAR ACTIVITIES*: Jack gets a haircut every month.

FUTURE:
TIMETABLES*: The train departs at 6:10 p.m. daily.
FUTURE IN TIME CLAUSES: He can't go until he finishes his homework.
WITH FUTURE TIME EXPRESSION: Classes start on Monday next week.

CONDITIONALS (IF): (See IF section.)
If it snows, I won't go to the party.
If you heat water to 100C, it boils.

* Often used with ADVERBS OF FREQUENCY: every week, sometimes, on Mondays, always, often, normally, usually, occasionally, rarely, seldom, never …

PAST SIMPLE

PAST:
FINISHED ACTIONS*: I ate dinner with my friend last night.
* Often used with time words: yesterday, this morning, last week, two years ago …
NEWS and DETAILS*: I broke my arm. I fell down.
* Often used following present perfect: I have broken my arm. I fell down.
ACTIONS IN STORIES: The girl sang and the audience clapped.

PRESENT / FUTURE:
IMAGINARY / UNREAL / UNLIKELY SITUATIONS:
If I won a million dollars, I would quit my job. (See IF section.)
I wish I had more money.

OTHER TENSES + PAST SIMPLE:
I've been out all morning (present perfect). I went shopping (past simple).

FUTURE SIMPLE

WILL > FUTURE PREDICTION:
Tom will be home by 6:45.

WILL > PROMISES / REQUESTS:
I will help you clean the house.
Will you please help me with my homework?

WILL > FUTURE CONDITIONALS (IF): (See IF section.)
If the weather is nice, we will go to beach.

BE GOING TO > PLANS / INTENTIONS:
I am going to London this summer.

BE GOING TO > FUTURE PREDICTIONS:
Sue is going to be rich and successful.

PRESENT CONTINUOUS

PRESENT:

UNFINISHED SHORT ACTIONS: Sally is studying at the moment.

TEMPORARY SITUATIONS NOW: They are living in Tokyo for a while.

TEMPORARY SITUATIONS LATER: Kenji is working tonight.

TEMPORARY HABITS: She's working a lot recently.

BAD HABITS: You're always complaining.

FUTURE:

DEFINITE PLANS: I am meeting my friends for dinner tonight.

* Most of these forms usually include a time expression.

PAST CONTINUOUS

SIMULTANEOUS ACTIONS (+ past simple): I was working when the mail arrived.

SIMULTANEOUS ACTIONS (+ while + past continuous): I was working while my mother was cooking dinner.

BACKGROUND INFORMATION: The dog was barking and the children were crying.

STRESSING THE LENGTH OF AN ACTION*: I was working at the office all day!

* Usually requires a time expression (for hours, all night, all week, etc.).

FUTURE CONTINUOUS

PLANS: She will be waiting for me at the airport.

PLANS + TIME: My father will be watching TV at 9:00 o'clock.

SIMULTANEOUS PLANS + WHEN + PRESENT SIMPLE: She will be waiting for me at the airport when I arrive.

POLITE INQUIRIES: When will be you leaving?

This form of inquiry is regarded as more polite than, "When will you leave?"

EXPECTED (USUAL) FUTURE PLANS: The students will be taking exams at the end of the year.

MODAL (AUXILIARY) VERBS

Can, could, should, shall, will, would, may, might, must, ought to. Unlike other verbs, their form never changes. These are helping verbs that provide more information about another verb. They indicate ability, necessity, possibility, and permission.

CAN > to express ability > I can drive.

COULD > to express possibility > We could try it and see.

SHOULD > to give advice > You should ask your mother.

SHALL > to offer > Shall I help you?

SHALL / WILL > to express obligation > You shall/will be home by 10:00 p.m., young man!

WOULD > to request > Would you please help me?

WOULD > to offer > Would you like some coffee?

MAY > to express possibility > The package may arrive tomorrow.

MAY > to request permission > May I please go first?

MIGHT > to express possibility > This might be the best hamburger ever!

MUST > to express obligation > The students must buy their textbooks.

MUST > to express a strong belief > You must have forgotten. I know I told you.

OUGHT TO > to suggest > You ought to buy the book. It will help you.

PRESENT PERFECT

FINISHED:

LIFE EXPERIENCES*: I have been to New York. I went there two years ago.
* Usually explained by a past simple sentence with a time expression.
UNFINISHED TIME BUT NOT ONGOING: Sally has not called me this week.
* Usually used with an uncompleted time expression, e.g. today, this evening, this year.
CURRENT SITUATION: He's lost his homework.
NEWS: The prime minister has met with the president.

UNFINISHED (the action is still ongoing):

LENGTH*: They have lived in Paris for 20 years.
HABITS: Emma has played piano since elementary school.
* Usually used with a time expression, e.g. since 2017, for 5 years/weeks/days.

NOTE: Present Perfect cannot be used with a completed time,
e.g. × Emily has been to the bank yesterday.

BEEN v. GONE

He's been to the supermarket. = He went, and he returned home. > finished action
He's gone to the supermarket. = He went, and he is still there. > unfinished action

PAST PERFECT

UNREAL/IMAGINED THINGS IN THE PAST:

I wish* I had studied English more.
* Usually used with: wish.

LENGTH OF TIME TO A POINT IN THE PAST:

Kana had been in Osaka for three years when she decided to return to Tokyo.
* Used with: time, when + past simple

ACTION/EVENT COMPLETED BEFORE ANOTHER PAST ACTION/EVENT:

When Shinji and Mariko arrived, the wedding had (already) started.
* The wedding started, then Shinji and Mariko arrived.
Alternatively, PAST SIMPLE + BEFORE:
The wedding started before Shinji and Mariko arrived.
When Hiroko graduated, she had been in Tokyo for five years.
* She lived in Tokyo for 5 years before she graduated. She may or may not still live there.

FUTURE PERFECT

LENGTH OF TIME TO A POINT IN THE FUTURE:

When she graduates from university, she will have lived in Tokyo for five years.
* Use with: when/by the time + present simple + will have + for + time

ACTION/EVENT COMPLETED BEFORE A POINT IN THE FUTURE:

By midnight, I will have finished my homework.
* Use with: by + time + will have
By the time I finish my homework, I will have studied for 6 hours.
* Use with: by the time + present simple, will have + time

PRESENT PERFECT CONTINUOUS

FINISHED:

CURRENT SITUATION: I've been exercising.
* Therefore, I am tired and sweaty, but I am finished exercising for today.

UNFINISHED:

LENGTH/DURATION: I've been living in Japan for 30 years.
* I am still living in Japan.

TEMPORARY SITUATION:

She's been going to the dentist frequently lately.
* She had a tooth problem, so she needs to see the dentist for a few weeks only.
* Use with: lately/recently

PAST PERFECT CONTINUOUS

LENGTH OF TIME TO A POINT IN THE PAST:

Kanako had been working at the company for 20 years when she became president.
* Use with: for + time, when + past simple

RESULT/OUTCOME/CONSEQUENCE AT A TIME IN THE PAST:

The garden was all white. It had been snowing.
The kitchen was a mess. The kids had been eating.
* The outcome is usually stated before the preceding cause.
* Use with: simple past

FUTURE PERFECT CONTINUOUS

LENGTH OF TIME TO A POINT IN THE FUTURE:

By next year, Mr. Takahashi will have been teaching for 30 years.
* Use with: by + time, for + time

ACTION/EVENT FINISHED BEFORE A POINT IN THE FUTURE:

When we meet up, I'll have been working (so I will be tired).
* Use with: when/by the time + simple present, (result/consequence)

IF

Zero Conditional:

Describes true situations. If = when or whenever.
e.g. If I go to the gym before work, I get up at 5:30 a.m.

First Conditional:

Refers to the present or future. Speculation about possible situations that can really happen.
e.g. If I study hard, I will pass my exams.

Second Conditional:

Refers to the present or future. Speculation about situations that will probably never happen.
e.g. If I won the lottery, I would quit my job.

Third Conditional:

Always refer to the past. Speculation about situations that happened or did not happen in the past.
e.g. If I had asked him, I would have known.

QUESTIONS / INTERROGATIVES

WH-questions
who, whom, whose, what, when, where, why, how, which, what kind of

Yes-No questions
do, does, did, is, are, was, were, have, has, had, can, could, will, would, may, might

Tag questions
Used after affirmative and negative sentences but not after questions.
… do you? … don't you? … is it? … isn't it? … have you? … haven't you? … am I?
NOTE: Negative tag questions are usually contracted, but non-contracted forms may be used in formal situations: e.g.
– You were in school at 10:00 a.m., weren't you? (informal)
– You were in school at 10:00 a.m., were you not? (formal)
– You weren't in school at 10:00 a.m., were you? (negative question, positive tag)

PARTS OF SPEECH: word types and categories

Noun (n.): a person, place, thing, or idea
e.g. Kyoko, teacher, school, money, love
Pronoun (pron.): a word in place of a noun
e.g. he, she, it, they, you, we
Verb (v.): a word that tells what someone or something does (actions)
e.g. jump, talk, listen, laugh, study
Adjective (adj.): a word used to describe (modify) a noun
e.g. happy, sad, green, fantastic, interesting, unbelievable
Adverb (adv.): a word used to describe (modify) a verb or an adjective, usually -ly
e.g. quickly, slowly, shyly, quietly, fast
Adverb of frequency (how often):
e.g. always, sometimes, often, usually, seldom, never
Preposition (prep.): a word used before a noun or pronoun to show location or movement
e.g. to, from, with, against, at, in, on, next to, under, behind, above, toward
Conjunction (conj.): a word or phrase used to connect/link other words and phrases
e.g. and, but, or, because, so, yet
Interjection (int.): a word used to express a sudden emotion, e.g. surprise or another strong feeling. Interjections can also be used on their own, e.g. Ouch! (in response to hitting your head).
e.g. Oh no!, My goodness!, Wow!, Yeah! Yes!, Gee!, Ah!, Brr!, Shh!
Article (art.): used to identify a subject (a noun)
Definite: the
e.g. The house on the street is for sale. = There is only one house on the street. It's for sale.
Indefinite: a/an
e.g. A house on the street is for sale. = There are many houses on the street. Only 1 is for sale.
Determiner (det.): words used before a noun to make it clear what the noun refers to
e.g. a/an/the/each/some/which/this/that/these/those/all/both/a few/a lot of/either/neither, and all pronouns (he/she/it) and possessive pronouns (his/hers/its)

Wow! Kaori and her new husband Kenji are happily enjoying their five-star honeymoon on the cruise ship.
Wow! (int.) Kaori and (conj.) her (pron.) new (adj.) husband (n.) Kenji are (v.) happily (adv.) enjoying (v.) their (pron.) five-star (adj.) honeymoon (n.) on (prep.) the (det.) cruise ship (n.).

Irregular Verbs

Root	Past	Past Participle
abide	abode	abode
arise	arose	arisen
awake	awoke	awoken
be	was/were	been
bear	bore	born
beat	beat	beaten
become	became	become
befall	befell	befallen
beget	begot	begotten
begin	began	begun
behold	beheld	beheld
bend	bent	bent
bereave	bereft	bereft
beseech	besought	besought
beset	beset	beset
bespeak	bespoke	bespoken
bestride	bestrode	bestridden
bet	bet	bet
bid	bade/bid	bidden/bid
bind	bound	bound
bite	bit	bitten
bleed	bled	bled
blow	blew	blown
break	broke	broken
breed	bred	bred
bring	brought	brought
broadcast	broadcast	broadcast
build	built	built
burn	burnt/burned	burnt/burned
burst	burst	burst
buy	bought	bought
can	could	—
cast	cast	cast
catch	caught	caught
choose	chose	chosen
cling	clung	clung
come	came	come
cost	cost	cost
creep	crept	crept
cut	cut	cut
deal	dealt	dealt
dig	dug	dug
do	did	done
draw	drew	drawn

Root	Past	Past Participle
dream	dreamt/dreamed	dreamt/dreamed
drink	drank	drunk
drive	drove	driven
dwell	dwelt/dwelled	dwelt/dwelled
eat	ate	eaten
interweave	interwove	interwoven
fall	fell	fallen
feed	fed	fed
feel	felt	felt
fight	fought	fought
find	found	found
flee	fled	fled
fling	flung	flung
fly	flew	flown
forbid	forbad(e)	forbidden
forecast	forecast	forecast
forget	forgot	forgotten
forgive	forgave	forgiven
forsake	forsook	forsaken
foresee	foresaw	foreseen
foretell	foretold	foretold
freeze	froze	frozen
get	got	got
give	gave	given
go	went	gone
grind	ground	ground
grow	grew	grown
hang	hung	hung
have	had	had
hear	heard	heard
hide	hid	hidden
hit	hit	hit
hold	held	held
hurt	hurt	hurt
keep	kept	kept
kneel	knelt/kneeled	knelt/kneeled
know	knew	known
lay	laid	laid
lead	led	led
lean	leant/leaned	leant/leaned
leap	leapt/leaped	leapt/leaped
learn	learnt/learned	learnt/learned
leave	left	left
lend	lent	lent

Root	Past	Past Participle
let	let	let
lie	lay	lain
lose	lost	lost
make	made	made
mean	meant	meant
meet	met	met
pay	paid	paid
mistake	mistook	mistaken
overhear	overheard	overheard
oversleep	overslept	overslept
put	put	put
read	read	read
rend	rent	rent
rid	rid	rid
ride	rode	ridden
ring	rang	rung
rise	rose	risen
run	ran	run
say	said	said
see	saw	seen
seek	sought	sought
sell	sold	sold
send	sent	sent
set	set	set
shake	shook	shaken
shed	shed	shed
shine	shone	shone
shit	shit/shat	shit/shat
shoot	shot	shot
show	showed	shown
shrink	shrank	shrunk
shrive	shrove	shriven
shut	shut	shut
sing	sang	sung
sink	sank	sunk
sit	sat	sat
slay	slew	slain
sleep	slept	slept
slide	slid	slid
sling	slung	slung
slink	slunk	slunk
slit	slit	slit
smell	smelt/smelled	smelt/smelled
smite	smote	smitten
speak	spoke	spoken
speed	sped	sped

Root	Past	Past Participle
spend	spent	spent
spin	spun	spun
spit	spat	spat
split	split	split
spoil	spoilt/spoiled	spoilt/spoiled
spread	spread	spread
spring	sprang	sprung
stand	stood	stood
steal	stole	stolen
stick	stuck	stuck
sting	stung	stung
stink	stank	stunk
stride	strode	stridden
strike	struck	struck
string	strung	strung
strive	strove	striven
swear	swore	sworn
sweep	swept	swept
swim	swam	swum
swing	swung	swung
take	took	taken
teach	taught	taught
tear	tore	torn
tell	told	told
think	thought	thought
throw	threw	thrown
thrust	thrust	thrust
tread	trod	trodden
understand	understood	understood
undertake	undertook	undertaken
undo	undid	undone
upset	upset	upset
wake	woke	woken
wear	wore	worn
weave	wove	woven
weep	wept	wept
win	won	won
wind	wound	wound
withdraw	withdrew	withdrawn
withstand	withstood	withstood
wring	wrung	wrung
write	wrote	written

Acknowledgments

What's That You Say? would not have been publishable without the support and cooperation of many good souls.

First and foremost, I am grateful to the entire team at Nan'un-do Publishing Co., Ltd. I am honored to have my textbook published by this esteemed publisher. More specifically, I am indebted to Hannah Hotta, editorial department, whose insights, encouragement, and patience helped shape the early stages of development. Chief Editor Atsushi Kato was equally gracious as he guided me through the middle and latter phases. They, and the book designers behind the scenes, made the entire process from manuscript submission to publication a pleasant endeavor.

I am also grateful to all the people who agreed to have their images published in this book: Alfred Chan, Beverley Price, Buddhika Sudarshana Gedara, Emi Tischler, Katerina Ruseva, Nat Shaffir, Darren Grusin, Kara Smit, Takashi Fujimoto (owner and head chef of Kyoryori Fujimoto, Kyoto), Juko Suzuki (Sokoninaru), UK folk band Bird in the Belly members: Jinnwoo, Tom Pryor, Adam Ronchetti, Laura Ward; and Paul McCartney/MPL Communications Ltd. UK.

Additionally, my gratitude to Miho Hotta for her Japanese translations, and to my friend and proofreader Owen T. Duggan for his feedback and insights. My thanks also to Anya Floris and Chris Koprowski for their beautiful readings of the unit texts. Sincere thanks also to those others who worked indirectly with me including proofreaders, designers, and office staff at Nan'un-do Publishing.

To one and all, thank you!

Jono David
Tokyo

What's That You Say? [B-944]
Bright Ideas for Reading, Writing, and Discussing in the English Classroom
自ら発信するための英語力養成講座

1刷　2023年1月9日

著　者　デイビッド・ジョノ　Jono David

発行者　南雲　一範　Kazunori Nagumo
発行所　株式会社　南雲堂
〒162-0801　東京都新宿区山吹町361
NAN'UN-DO Co., Ltd.
361 Yamabuki-cho, Shinjuku-ku, Tokyo 162-0801, Japan
振替口座 : 00160-0-46863
TEL:　03-3268-2311（営業部：学校関係）
03-3268-2384（営業部：書店関係）
03-3268-2387（編集部）
FAX:　03-3269-2486

編集者　加藤　敦／堀田　華

組　版　柴崎　利恵

装　丁　銀月堂

日本語試訳　堀田　三穂

検　印　省　略

コード　ISBN978-4-523-17944-3　C0082

Printed in Japan

E-mail : nanundo@post.email.ne.jp
URL : https://www.nanun-do.co.jp/